FOR THE HEARING OF THE TALE, FOR THE FUTURE OF THE WISH

Hilda Meers

*With best wishes
from Hilda*

COUNTRY BOOKS

Published by:
Country Books
Courtyard Cottage, Little Longstone, Bakewell, Derbyshire DE45 1NN
Tel/Fax: 01629 640670
e-mail: dickrichardson@country-books.co.uk

ISBN 1 898941 77 7

COVER ILLUSTRATION:
from a private collection.

THE AUTHOR

Hilda Meers grew up in the Midlands, where being a child of Jewish immigrant parents in the thirties' slump was not a lot of fun. She began writing stories when she worked as a factory 'hand', but married and acquired two children before adding on poetry during her teacher-in-training time. Special-school teaching and a ground-breaking book on language acquisition, '*Helping Our Children Talk*' (published by Longmans) led to teaching child development to intending teachers; on her retirement a short-term job in Jordan led to an unusual novel, '*The Blood Tie*' (published by Citron Press). Now in North-East Scotland, her short stories have appeared in magazines, including '*The Broken Fiddle*' (published by Aberdeenshire Council) and '*The Leopard*', her poems in '*Deliberately Thirsty*' (published by Thirsty Books, Edinburgh), in two issues of '*Pushing Out the Boat*' (Aberdeenshire Council) and in '*Second Light*'. Also published is a story, '*Acts of Love*', Making Waves Publications. Her recent research has resulted in a book '*For the Hearing of the Tale, For the Future of the Wish*', which focuses on the little-known opposition, sabotage and resistance which took place within the concentration camps and prisons of the Nazi era.

THE BOOK

Against the humiliation and despair designed by an arrogant system and its corrupted administrators, rose the indomitable spirit of those at the very edge of what it is possible for human beings to endure. Of many nations and faiths, whether notable or ordinary, overcoming differences of nationality and political attitudes, they joined together, hands, minds, strengths, weaknesses, all: to create chinks of free thought, sing songs, strive for life – these men and women, dying or surviving, are worthy of our remembrance, their stories relevant to the way each of us lives life now.

'For the Hearing of the Tale, For the Future of the Wish' creatively combines fictional characters who present true stories, first that of a jailed journalist's political opposition during the Nazi occupation of Czechoslovakia.

Highlights from German history – post-1918, the Weimar period, the rise of Nazism, illumine the dark background of the period, setting the scene for accounts of organised resistance, highly secret, undertaken by the diverse occupants of the many concentration camps. For not all of those who died in the gas chambers went there 'like lambs to the slaughter'; wherever possible determined men and women blew up crematoria, sabotaged work vital for the German war machine (including damaging Vl and V2 rockets), escaped to join partisan groups or to bring out evidence proving to the world what was happening in the camps.

Above all they organised to save many fellow-prisoners' lives – astounding escapes, brilliant technicians, daring and self-sacrifice – this book relates many little-known tales, compiled from archival sources, memoirs, diaries.

While in this account the narrators Mr Julius and Arthur Milne, also Jane, Simon, his Uncle and his Grandfather are invented characters, all other persons and events are drawn from historical sources (referred to in the text where appropriate and acknowledged in the Bibliography).

CONTENTS

FOR THE HEARING OF THE TALE, FOR THE FUTURE OF THE WISH

THE START OF THE TALE

It began that May Day. I never dreamed, then, that I'd get in so deep.

All I'd done was to go into that café – how was I to know, then, Mr Julius would turn, would see me, would single me out? I know I'm about to make a fool of myself, stood up here clutching my notes, sweating, facing students already sniffing their next-year degrees – being introduced now, as Mr Milne, our speaker for today – our speaker! Our fish out of water, more like.

What's up with that young scraggy-looking chap sat near the front, whispering to the girl beside him, her pale skin, luminous eyes, him jumping up, specs, bony cheekbones – a convulsive swallow lumping his adam's apple. Demand in his thin questioning voice:

'Have you always taken an interest in the special subject of, er, resistance to the Nazis in political prisons and concentration camps? Have you research qualifications?'

He can't credit an uneducated person's interests. Special subject? Not to my mind, not like horticulture, that's my special subject. I hear myself say, 'No, indeed, it's only recently I found out anything about such matters.'

I put my lecture notes down on the table-top, possessed by the need to explain how I got drawn in:

'Let me tell you how I met Mr. Julius. I was on my way to the Garden Centre. I stopped off at the Broch when it started to rain. Hard, stinging rain. I ducked into a café. A man outside, darkly-dressed, very ancient, very bent, pushing a shopping trolley - not a supermarket trolley, one of those check-patterned affairs, with four wheels. He'd an unusual way of getting along, back bent, face hung over the trolley handle. Quick, determined steps. Like a purposeful bird.

'He came into the cafe breathing hard, a puff of roll-up tobacco and wet wool from his overcoat wafting in with him. He shook off the raindrips. Fetched a mug of coffee, sat down at my table. How peculiar he looked, close to! A nose that'd seen better days, if its sideways and misshapen appearance told a true tale. Eyes – his eyes looked through you.

'His veined and liverspot-blotched hands, the fingers out at odd angles, as if, as if they couldn't manage to agree amongst themselves which way they should point. With his breath wheezing out, he commented, "Each day a gift – though the coffee is ersatz." And something made me say, "It's a long time since I've heard that word, although I'm old enough to remember Hitler" – and I added, "And concentration camps."

'He swirled the coffee round inside his mug. Bird-bright eyes on me, while he hunted for, chose careful words. "Perhaps you notice, my English is not quite as a native speaker would command it. My country of birth, that was Czechoslovakia. Now its name is a history, its present state of being, the Czech Republic, which is – as it is. I visit a younger sister here in Fraserburgh. I do so for several months each year."

'I told him – exchange of information, a usual courtesy — that I stayed in a bungalow, with a pleasant outlook, a comfortable bachelor-style life. No close family. A fixed existence. Luckily an untroubled one, a good life.

'The man's glittery old eyes sparkled amusement while he commented, "That, perhaps, is something that may possibly change."

'I didn't follow him. Silences seem so long, when they occur in an attempted conversation with a stranger. Do you find that? I couldn't just move away, though the rain had lessened.

'His stiff, slightly accented voice started up again. "There is a man I think about. A man called Julius. That was his first name, the name I spoke with him by. When the war ended I traveled to several countries before I came, first to England, now to Scotland. Also I changed my name, not my given name, you understand, but my second. So now I am Mr. Julius."

'I told him my own name, adding, "You must have thought a lot of your friend Julius, to take the same name."

'"Julius? Ach, he was stupid, stupid! So much risk he took, as if he was immortal. True, he was strong as a tree. A man of talent, a writer. Such love of life … he wished always to be remembered as a man who lived his life for joy. He wanted, no sadness should be attached to his name."

'He fell silent, and I thought of a set of garden pots I'd intended to buy, at Mintlaw, just a few miles away. You might think garden pots aren't important, but they were a part of my cherished plan for the patio where I sit with a glass of malt on a fine summer evening, watching the sunset. Well anyway I used to.

'"Before the first war," he went on, "Julius was at school, I, just starting. His father had work at the factory, you will have heard of Skoda cars? We grew up. Julius took other paths. I never thought to meet him again."

'The old man leaned forward, pulled out a large handkerchief, wiped his mouth before telling me of Julius throwing in his lot with "the political struggles of the working people". I had to ask what this meant, and that encouraged Mr. Julius to give me a history lesson:

'"Bohemia! A great kingdom once, in medieval days, you understand. Then came the Thirty Years War. Perhaps you have not heard of the Battle of the White Mountain? No, I thought perhaps not. That was in 1620. It sealed our fate – in time after that we were subject to Austria. By order of the Emperor Joseph, we Czechs were not allowed for the children to have even school-books in our own language. Then the war in 1914. Following that, the Russian Revolution, 1917. In 1918, October 28th, what a day! The Czechoslovak Republic proclaimed, independence for our country. I hoped to become a doctor, a musician even, but my parents were poor. With a wife and family in the course of time, I must be practical, not political about my work. But Julius, now a journalist. did not like the regime.

'"Julius Fucik edited nine illegal news sheets and periodicals, he and his wife joined the banned Communist Party. Those two innocents deeply believed Communism would bring in a lifetime of song, of sunshine, above all of freedom. That was the future of their wish. Fascism he hated, he set all his strength, his active brain, against it. Six months before the Munich agreement, men like Julius, women like his wife Gusta, became hunted people."

'Mr. Julius began to hum, a folk-song sort of sound that made the other people in the café turn round and look. A young woman with two children in tow stared at us as she wove her way to the door. I dare say we looked odd, sitting with our heads together like latter-day conspirators, talking about communists. In those days, I felt embarrassed if I did anything to stand out of the crowd.

'Well, he went on talking. His words hissed across the table – revealing to my imagination a large room — six long benches arranged in rows one behind the other, shabby brown-painted wooden backs towards me. In front of them, a blank wall, yellowish in colour, blotched here and there with ill-defined smudges. This wall, lit by harsh overhead lighting, is all that can be seen by the two men seated rigidly upright on separate benches, unmoving, hands pressed close to their knees. They stare straight ahead at the yellowish wall as if it's a screen on which an absorbing film is showing.

'At one side of the room, near one of two doors, stands a tall man wearing a uniform. Is it to show his power, his contempt, his hatred, or even his fear, that he curls his lip as he surveys the half-rags of stained clothing, the gaunt and grey-skinned men with the pallor of creatures who have been shut away from air and sunshine, whereas he is smart, well groomed, well shod with well-polished shoes?

'Only uneven breathing-sounds, louder as seconds pass, are heard in that room. Then a crash as the door swings open, another man is half-pushed, half-dragged in. He's tall, powerfully built. His bare, bruised feet are swollen. The two gaunt men do not look at him as he is pushed onto the bench – and yet their eyes seem to slide sideways for a brief moment. A moment only; but in that moment the newcomer – Julius Fucik – rapidly blinks, once, twice, and on his battered face a twitch of his swollen lip makes response to the once, twice, blinking of the weary and wary souls who sit there so rigidly upright, facing the yellowish wall, hands pressed close to their knees.

'One of the seated men is grabbed, pulled upright, propelled through the other door, a desk is glimpsed, a man seated behind it. And heavy men with heavy sticks. Heavy voices shout "Speak! We know everything, speak! Speak!" The door shuts, the two waiting men strain forward, hear the sounds – blows, groans, yells of "Talk! Tell us their names! Speak!" The man who went in there walking is carried out, unconscious. The man with the bruised and swollen feet stares calmly at the yellowish wall.

'Within the interrogation room, the sweating uniformed men pause, take a refreshing drink of water. One with alert intent eyes gestures to the other, who does his bidding cringingly.

'The cringing man says, "These Communists! They keep their mouths shut, they don't even feel pain, they're more stupid than animals."

'The tall man shrugs, replies in a clipped, acidulous voice, "We must try again with Fucik. A member of the Executive of the Czechoslovak Communist Party, when he gives us the names of his comrades, as he calls them, what propaganda! What about bringing in his wife again, eh?"

'Here Mr Julius paused to fetch more coffee. My eyes were watering. I blew my nose, using the clean white handkerchief I keep handy in my jacket pocket. I found myself senselessly wondering, how would a person get by if they were arrested and hadn't got a clean handkerchief on them?'

'Mr Julius told me then of Mrs Fucik, saying, "His wife, Gusta, later she was sent to Ravensbrück. Some who were very determined, a few even more determined who showed us how not to succumb, those whose luck held, chance weaving its web with necessity, these survived the concentration camps. Only later did I learn, after I found Gusta Fucikova, just how much I, and many many more, owe to unknown friends who helped us live on.

'Mr. Julius' bluish lips twisted into – not a smile, not even an ironic one. It struck me as being more like a physical shudder at the thought of what our species has shown itself capable of doing – not only in that prison, not only in those concentration camps. Pensively, he withdrew one of the paper napkins from the container that stood at the corner of the table; neatly controlling his divergent fingers, he wiped coffee-froth from the corners of his mouth. I was hypnotised, I could only wait for him to go on, which he very soon did:

'"Julius, when he was caught at a friend's flat, was disguised, a beard, a limp, as a Professor Horak. He knew, if he should try to get away, the owners of the flat would certainly be killed, whereas if he did not act to save himself, probably they would only get a prison sentence."

'"He sacrificed himself?" I asked. Mr Julius' eyebrows twitched. I daresay he decided I was very naïve, but he only said, "I would not put it quite like that myself. Say rather, he saved his self-respect. That can not be said for another man there that night. But the man whose flat it was, Mr Joseph Jelinek, with his wife Mary Jelinek – that was the name – gave the Gestapo no information. She found a way to send out her last bidding. This artless woman, what would she have to say, do you think, worthy of remembrance? Simply, she wanted no-one to feel sorry for her, no-one should get scared, all her life she'd done her duty as a worker – she would die like that too."

'"What about her husband, Joseph?" I asked Mr Julius in the space he collected breath in. And I remember, I swear it, every word he said. It went like this: "Joseph. A simple ordinary man. The interrogators beat him, and beat him more; he did not speak. Not until Julius, who was at that time almost dead, recovered enough to show him, by word, by look, what or how he might answer to lead the Gestapo astray. No more is known, of the wife, or the husband, or many such people. But I must return to Julius, it is of him I must speak. What the Gestapo never understood was that Julius so loved life. Above all he loved people, he joyed in song, always he sang when they dragged him back to his cell. And when he learned – for a prison has many voices, many whispers, many walls that can be tapped on to send a message that will hearten, will strengthen a person in utmost extremity –- even the warders were not all heartless – wait, I tell you of one warder, an honest Czech man, who had heard that Julius Fucik was a writer. This man, what did he do? He took a great, an enormous risk. He brought to Julius, paper and pen. He understood, a writer, what he needs is to write.

'Julius made sure it was not a trap, not till then would he write. Each sheet of paper smuggled out, hidden away until better times. I have read those pages, for Gusta, when she was liberated out of Ravensbrück – that camp was liberated on the first day of May, 1945 – yes, that is right, by chance it was on May Day, she began her search for Julius. Round the comrades went Gusta, collecting the numbered pages one by one. How must she have felt when she read those lines when he writes of their great love for each other, praises her steadfastness, tells – when he learned from the tapped-out messages that she was in Pancrac prison too, in the women's cells on the floor below his – how each night he sang, hoping she would hear him and know he lived.

'"Those scattered pages have been printed. Gusta Fucikova saw to that. But you, I see, know nothing of what Julius achieved inside that hellish prison. The "collective" he developed there, he wrote of that. As you will have guessed, I was there myself for a time, before they tired of me and sent me to the concentration camp for a holiday there."

'To describe Mr. Julius's expression, I'd say it was a mirthless grin. People speak of a mirthless grin, don't they. If you've never seen one, I can tell you, when you do, you feel your flesh crawl. Anyway, he pushed up his sleeve, the left one, to show a row of small blue numbers, there were six, a seventh that was a letter, tattooed onto the inner forearm, while he said, "My badge of honour."

'Rolling down his sleeve again, over the cheap-looking watch he wore – the leather of the strap was all cracked and broken –- I caught a whiff of the smell of his skin, not like any other smell I could think of, except that – if a ghost had a smell, it would be like the smell of the skin on Mr. Julius's arm. He trotted to the counter for yet anothes coffee. I hadn't realised before, that if his back hadn't been out of its natural shape, he'd have been a tall man.

'I tried to put my thoughts in order. The tale sounded over-dramatic, the high-minded high-flown idealists resisting to an incredible degree. How could Mr. Julius know so much about it? And why was he insisting on telling it all to me now, all these years later, and long after it had stopped raining?

'Mr. Julius' account didn't spare me the details. Julius truly believes he takes part in the last battle for the freedom of man. A young fellow-prisoner, Karel Marlik, had worked in an ore mine near Hudlice until he'd been caught smuggling out explosives. Karel, in the cell with Julius, nursed him after the torture sessions. One night Karel was taken out. Before the guard could lead him away, Karel knelt down by Julius' palliase, put his arms round him, kissed him. In the corridor, a uniformed warder who watched let out a rasping cry.

'Mr. Julius paused, looking out into the street, the pale blue of April's sky. "Oh look, it's stopped raining!" I exclaimed – with a false air of surprise. I should have known Mr. Julius wouldn't be distracted from his tale, and he wasn't.

'"Yes, I have noticed," he sneered, "We will continue, if you please." And something held me there, though it would soon be too late to go to the garden centre for the pots. I'd been looking forward, you know, to planting them out at the weekend. Nostalgically, I suppose – considering … but I had to hear about other prisoners, before he told me of the trial – and of what took place after that.

'Joseph Pesek was a teacher, known as 'Dad'. In cell 267, he too nursed Julius. They sing together, talk together. During the half-hour allowed for exercise in the courtyard, this Dad, like a true father, takes an amazing great risk for son Julius. He picks for him a daisy, and a blade of grass.

'I was confused. Mr Julius was telling me more than a fellow-prisoner might be expected to know. But when I asked him about how Julius got the chance to write, he said the trustworthy warder, a man called Kolinsky, from an old family in Moravia, had registered as a German so he could work as a guard in the prisons where Czechs were held. Some guards like him did help prisoners, others gave only blows, from their own fear. More than one warder of the cringing kind said, according to Mr Julius, "If I didn't work here, I'd have only twenty crowns to keep my family on. Twenty crowns, it's not enough! And if I didn't do it, somebody else would, it would make no difference. And others would do it worse than I do – I only do what I'm told to do, I only beat the prisoners when they're too obstinate to speak, or when the Gestapo is watching. So I eat, I have a place to stay, I don't want war, I don't want people to die, I just want to live myself, and not be bothered with all this politics." And he added,

'"As well as the warders, who were Germans, at least …" He'd hesitated before going on, squirming about a bit as though the seat had suddenly become uncomfortable, "I will explain for you, most warders were Germans, there were some Czech prison officers, even one or two Czech interpreters and medical orderlies. When they were short of men, they had to bring in Czechs as warders. Then the prisoners knew things looked bad for the German Army. Prisoner-orderlies take food to the cells, do other duties. Can you imagine the risk to them? They are the smugglers of messages between cells, between prison and the outside world, those the guards decided were reliable enough, isolated enough, to sweep corridors at their bidding! Skorepa was one who won their praise for his quietness, his reliable work habits. And all the time he studied them, studied the prisoners too, for to help the prisoners he must know strengths and weaknesses that can be used, built on, how to respond shrewdly and flexibly as situations arise, wariness and presence of mind all put to one end, to do the duty as he perceives it, of giving exact reports, of giving strength to the man who needs the sight of a friend's kind eyes as much as he needs the smuggled little loaf, bread to tide him over the worst patches. That was how it was in the prison; and so too in the concentration camp."

'"That chap Skorepa sounds like an example to all the orderlies," I muttered, not caring to add, that all the same, like Julius, he sounded somewhat too good to be true. Mr Julius remarked dryly, "He must be very secret about his unusual abilities. Few would notice, indeed they must not notice, for in the majority of people – yes, I include myself among that majority – there is a mixture, of the brave and the cowardly, firm sometimes, helpful to others sometimes, but at other times weak like a cringing dog, eyes meanly snatching at the other's bread. Risk came from many quarters, the fellow-feeling of the prisoners was after all balanced on many chances. It was possible to tell whether the news from the front was good or bad – a little extra bread, or a bowl of soup, if the warders thought Germany was losing the war, so that prisoners, some of them, might survive to speak of the good treatment that a warder had doled out like the watery soup. What else but this conglomeration could you expect from us, are we not all children of our time – though Julius might regard himself as a child of future times. But, who knows?"

'The old man's shoulders rise in a shrug, hands turned outwards, palm upwards, lower lip pushed out, curled down, an age-old gesture. He seemed uneasy, and hurriedly continued: "After eighteen months they moved Julius to Berlin to be tried. The charges were, plotting against the integrity of the Reich and of preparing an armed rising and revolution."

'The Court hearing began at 9 a.m. on the morning of August 25th 1943. The President of the Court was Roland Freisler, a name I came across again, much later, in the record of another trial, with a different outcome.

'Mr Julius said, he recalled the proceedings. "Wait, wait," I implored him. "Mr Julius, a person would have to be present at the trial to know about it."

'He was unshakeable. "Quite so, quite so, indeed. I was there. I am sure you have been wondering about that." He was meeting my gaze with his own, holding me. There was something odd, so odd it gave me a shrinking sense of horror that baffled my understanding. I tried again. "You mean, you were on trial with him?"

'"No. Not, at anyrate, in the way you mean. In another way, perhaps, yes. Wait, very soon now I will explain myself, your questions will find answers. For a moment more, please allow me to continue. I must speak!"

'As if each phrase he jerked out cost him as much pain as a pulled-out tooth, he did go on: "The death penalty. Was. Demanded by. The prosecutor, a man by the name. Of Nobel. Also. By the defending counsellor, a Herr Hoffman. In Germany these things must be done correctly. According to law. The prisoner must. Have a defending counsel, even though he doesn't get to see him before they first size each other up in the courtroom."

'Using, not the big handkerchief he'd used for his eyes, but one of those paper napkins cafés supply, Mr Julius blew his sideways-shifted nose, elaborately. He leaned forward, eyes fierce. "Julius insisted he would speak, now at last he would speak, though hard indeed they tried to stop him. I, I was in the court, I heard him, in a long speech, he passed sentence on them… The Nazis had sent me from Pancrac to interpret at the trial, for I spoke both German and Czech languages, I had worked for them in Prague as a medical orderly, as an interpreter, I was not a prisoner, not part of the Pancrac collective, not a bad man either, or so I thought, but a weight was on me, the weight of knowing I had cringed, I had said, I only follow the orders, if I don't someone else will, it's just a job, I have to eat. And I heard Julius, all marked and scarred, raise his voice above the shouting stamping rage of the President of the Court: "Life to man!" he calls out. "The future to Communism," he adds for good measure. By midday it was over. A farce, if a farce may also be tragic. Next day, to Plotenzee prison to await the death sentence. I was sent with him – by this time the Reich was short of manpower for guards, even a renegade Czech like myself was put to their use.

'"The sentence, death by hanging, would be carried out on September 8th, at 4.55 in the morning. Julius told them, he knew why they cut short the usual one hundred days between trial and death. They feared the Russians (at that time, if you remember, the Soviet Union was, as Mr. Churchill said, our gallant ally in the fight against Hitler) they feared the Allied armies might reach Berlin before all the prisoners could be executed. They feared this too for the concentration camps, Himmler himself wrote the order that all the prisoners in all the camps were to be exterminated, gassed, shot when they fell exhausted on forced evacuation marches."

'Mr Julius had to pause, wipe the sweat from his face, before he could go on: "And so in the early morning, the SS men came, and led Julius from his cell, along the corridors to the place of execution. I was assigned to walk behind him, there might be some last words in need of translation. Or perhaps they wanted to show a Czech their power. Who knows? Certainly, they showed this Czech person their power, in that prison and in the death camp too. For the Gestapo and the SS arrested me in my turn, as a man they wished to teach a lesson to – I learned lessons indeed but of a different character from those they intended me to learn. One of the important things I learned, in the prison and more especially in the concentration camp, is that it is not a question of this nation, or of that. It is everywhere. Nor was it only then, in that place and of that time. The rhetoric of "obey" still curdles the blood, even as today the power-mad salute the bombs, the guns, the machetes that spill it. Army commanders frame their orders, politicians clothe the soldiers in the uniforms of battle. The marvellous technology of the world is deployed, bringing satisfaction to the owners and shareholders of the armaments factories, the arms smugglers, company directors who rub their hands at the thought of profitable contracts to be had for the rebuilding of the demolished bridges, the burnt-out houses, all, all who ensure – who ensure murderous hate continues. Who ensure life is stifled, and devastation is our whirlwind. The Goebbels-style manipulation, the cynical distortions of the meaning of words, the twisted images for re-assurance of the peoples, become the false sound-bites uttered; seized on by those who feel comforted on hearing them, pap easily chewed, morsels swallowed down, gulp, gulp, no need to think or work the situation out for ourselves – and people console themselves, there is anyway nothing to be done. If we know ninety-one countries still use torture, should that not wrench at our capacity to deny, melt our secret wish to turn away from those who see, who bear witness? Well, I saw. I became, however unwillingly, myself a witness."

'He breathed hard and long, this old, old relic of a man, his face indescribably twitching. After a false start or two, he got going again: "Julius held himself straight, he walked firmly along the corridor to death. In his powerful voice, he began to sing. That song, I had heard it many times before, issuing from cell 267, Julius singing, at first his mouth so smashed I could hardly make out the words, and Dad Pesek, all out of tune, he couldn't even keep in the right key – and young Karel's voice, making it a trio, hopeful and mournful both, an old tune transformed to a new composition in the mode appropriate to the time and the place. Hearing that song wrenched me back to the night when they took Karel away to be tried and condemned. Yes, it was I who was in the corridor that night, on duty outside the cell, as that young man turned to Julius, who could not yet rise from the stinking mattress. As I have told you, Karel knelt down by the man he'd nursed, the man who had helped him with song, with cheerful looks, with firm belief; and as Karel kissed him, there in the prison where there was no place for love, so the Fascists thought – a cry burst from me – how long since anyone in the world cared enough about me to show such simple unselfconscious love?

"'For I had not earned it. I felt as though a hand gripped my heart. That was the beginning, for me, of the feeling that a weight dragged at me, a weight growing, clutching, something that was beyond me to fathom. And in the early morning when Julius must walk that corridor to his death, in his love of life, he sang. But it is not in prison regulations that prisoners should sing as they are marched off to execution. The SS guards were scandalised, they seized him, roughly bound his mouth shut. Still he held himself straight. It was then – from somewhere in that prison, prisoners who had heard him began themselves to sing, they took up the song Julius sang at the point where his own voice was muffled, and they sang, with all their hearts they sang!

"And I, though I had been myself a lackey for the SS – I felt, then, something snap within me; in a split second, I decided, and as I too raised my voice to take up the soaring chorus of the song, friend, it was as though that inner weight dropped from me. For it was my choice to defy, to sing, not you understand because it was my duty, and not even any more as a Czechoslovak citizen asserting his national identity. I sang with the determined wish to act as a free human being. I sang with love for those who sowed the seeds of a free life, a peaceful life in the unknown future. It dawned on me then, that the small acts of fellowship that make up the ethos of "a collective" are neither more nor less than the practical daily expressions of such love."

'Mr Julius wiped a trace of spittle from his lips. With the big handkerchief. That odd smile from him, before he said, with some rancour, "How corny? Perhaps, perhaps not. Anyway, not so long after that, when the Gestapo and the SS had got tired beating me, I was not a tall man any more, I no more had a face that would attract a woman, and, for me worse than that, my fingers would never again coax music from a violin. If I had known anything that was of use to them, it was when they broke each of my fingers, one by one, that I might – who knows – I might have spoken. After my trial, the prisons at that time being overfull, I was sent on to a concentration camp. It was fortunate for me that I knew German, the language used for shouting out the orders. Those who did not could be dead before their understanding had the chance to inform them of the meanings of the coarse German phrases used.

"'First", said Mr Julius, "The understanding: from the entry through its gates, if you wish to live, rules must be instantly, unquestionably obeyed. To look fit for work. Not to hit back. To get through the selection process, how did I do that, misshapen as I was? That, I learned later, when I spoke with Gusta Fucikova."

"'The camps, though they differ in size, or how near to factories in need of such slave workers as we became – all, all most admirably designed to kill, by extinction through overwork, by hunger or despair, by beatings and shootings – stripped, pushed into the overworked gas chambers, burned in ovens, pitiful remnants of what once were people, now beyond their pain; death by humiliation, destruction of all human dignity. Not one prisoner must escape, for even if caught and brought back to be hanged, still they have shown, Nazis are not the source of all strength and will."

'Mr. Julius, I learned, was set to work. Lorded over by a prisoner wearing an armband with a green triangle stitched to it. A green triangle meant you were there as a criminal. Political prisoners had red triangles, the 'anti-socials' black. Homosexual prisoners had a pink triangle. Gypsies had brown, Jehovah's Witnesses purple. Jews two yellow triangles, one across the other, a Star of David. Jews and Russian prisoners-of-war got the harshest treatment. By the twisted Nazi ideology, these were sub-human. Mr Julius described for me seeing Jews, old men, thin as laths, harnessed to carts loaded with the already dead, that they must pull to the crematorium for burning. The pink triangle men were given a hard time, in ways I will not describe.

'It was Mr Julius' luck only to be classed as a criminal. His task, to carry heavy rocks. As he told me. Each one carried from spot A to spot B must then be carried back, from B to A. The kapo, a fellow-prisoner with an armband giving him authority, found this amusing. Stooges of the camp administration had such power, so long as the beds in the barracks were neatly made and work assignments met. If a beating went too far and a prisoner died, no great shakes. All the kapo did was to alter the numbers on the roll call. Morning and night the roll call. Mr Julius said, wryly, "Perhaps I, too, would soon have died. But this kapo made some mistake, he upset the SS administration. Perhaps he got the numbers wrong, perhaps he stole too blatantly, who knows? At any rate, his armband taken from him, he became once more as the rest of us, he must sleep too in the same barracks room we huddled in at night. And that night, during the night, scuffling sounds, padding of bare feet, whispers, a gurgling noise – in the morning, his dead body in the bunk."

'The next kapo wore a red armband, the beatings lessened. Mr Julius was transferred, to work at keeping the camp kitchens clean. Most of his fellow-workers wore red triangles. Some were German, some Austrian. Luckily he could speak to them in their language.

'He told me, "From Pancrac I had already learned the trade of a thief, how to steal food, how to hide some article that can be traded for food, how not to be caught. In the camps there was little time for learning such needful arts of survival. But more, much more, my friend, did I need ."'

'He was coughing quite badly, struggling for breath – he really was very old. The café had emptied out its customers. A young woman in a checked apron wiped the tables down; from the kitchen came the clatter of crockery, washed-up and being put away. "It is nearly all said," he remarked ironically.

"So, what else is there, that's needed?" I prompted him.

'"Take an example. We are near starving, I am skin, bone. In the hut at night, shivering as I lie on stinking straw, near despair I hear a voice, a whisper, "Hold on." I look around, no-one stirs. Beside me, what is this? I pick it up, it is a piece of a potato, two strings of meat cling to it, it has been placed near my hand. How can I die now? To die would be a waste of the magnificent gift, it would be to deny the courage of he who stole it – I hold it in my mouth, let its precious nourishment slowly, slowly dissolve. I swallow. And I know by this means what to do. I steal from the kitchen where I go to work, a small loaf of bread is mine. Do I hide away, secretly eat? No. I divide the loaf, such a pitifully small loaf, into smaller pieces, mouthfuls only. I look around me. I remember the warder who observed strength, weakness, to know who needs his help, and I make a friend, the first I share with, soon we each give to the other. Then there are others, whom I pick out as being in greatest need at that moment – but can I trust them to be secret? This too I must decide. And for those for whom I have not bread left, there can be a look given, of understanding, the look that says, "Hold on." For the clamour of the first hunger pangs are the worst for a man to endure, before his stomach has shrunk, his body adapted … did you know, my friend, that it is the big, the well-built well-nourished ones who suffer most, in those first weeks? Their bodies do not have the trick of making do with little food, the lean ones who already know privation fare better when they must make do with one litre of watery soup, a little bread, a mug of something that may be tea or perhaps it is coffee, who can tell, and still must look fit for work. The collective of the prison became the collective of the camps. To be alone, that is death – inside the camp, or out of it. Marching music – the camp band was made to play as the work details set off to their daily work in the armaments factories – this kept us alive too, it reminds us that outside this hellish world of the camp, with its beatings, its killing, another world – some of the prisoners, at night, would devise mathematical systems in their heads, or speak to invisible students on German literature, philosophy – if you listened, there was an education to be obtained from the skeletal professors; one man in my block recited to himself, in English, which I did not know at that time, long poems he had learned. Sometimes, at great risk, a letter would be smuggled out, an answer received – I have heard a saying, about keeping body and soul together. Once the soul gave up, the body could no longer survive until the gates would swing open."

'He gave me time to think that over, seemingly impervious to the hard looks of the waitress, who would have preferred us gone. Then he was off again, rattling away with his tale: "And since you ask, my friend, I will tell you more. When we were liberated – that was in 1945 – those of us who were not quite dead saw the faces of the Allied soldiers turn grey and pale, they held handkerchiefs over their noses, some turned away to vomit – we could go wherever we chose.

'"After I had taught my stomach to accept food again, I set out to find if anyone was left of my family, or of those I used to know. In this way, I learned new skills, the skills of a wanderer on the face of the earth. I traced Gusta. Ravensbrück, the first camp built for women prisoners, as I learned from her, had begun its career some time between April 1938 and the start of the war in 1939. On April 21st 1945, the SS had begun to evacuate it – the Russian army arrived on May 1st. To the joy of those still able to feel joy. More did not, their homes, their families were vanished like smoke. I told Gusta of the end her husband made. She spoke of his journal and thanked me for not betraying any knowledge to the Gestapo. She thanked me, I tell you, and it was like a blow. You have an expression, I think, the heaping coals of fire on the head?"

'"Gusta's thought was that people must know what had passed, that we who had survived must inform future times, help to create Julius' wish of the future, its dignity, freedom, joy, its songs. She it was who told me of prisoners who, very secretly, grouped together, they organised resistance within hell itself, getting news out to the world of what was done to us, writing and hiding the records of our suffering and our resistance. Also sabotage taking place in the factories where we of the striped uniforms were set to work to help the German war effort. Above all else, the task to save all who could be saved, for it was not true, not true, that we went 'like sheep to the slaughter', though little enough could we do, for ourselves or our fellow men and women."

'He brooded awhile, before softly and pensively adding, "Now our present has caught up with the time Julius visualised as the future, we can see that all did not turn out as he would have wished. But I wonder – if Julius and his like had lived, perhaps they could have created differently? Even, perhaps, as Mandela? Life has many futures, it is seeded in many ways. I, too, had a responsibility to the future, if I truly wished to amend my weak and paltry past. This will amuse you. I had the curiosity to find out, what was the poem that the man in the bunk above mine recited to keep his sanity in the chill of the night-time, a strange poem, about a man all at sea, who commits an evil act. For this he must do penance, by teaching the lesson from his life, to those who will benefit from hearing it.

'I stared then, as you can imagine. I knew from my schooldays, the poem he spoke of. He nodded his head three times, gave me his quizzical look; "So. I know what I must do with the life remaining to me. I travelled, from country to country.

My keen musician's ear helped me learn languages – to learn most languages, to speak them well enough for my purpose, was not hard. I had my bread to earn too, which was inconvenient, for it limited my opportunities to journey to other lands. I pledged myself to do so, at least once in each year that passed, and for as long as I can. Now, especially as May Day approaches, and my friend, tomorrow, Saturday, is the last May Day of this present century, is it not? When the workers' processions of Julius' remembrance would wind through the streets and fill the squares of Prague with parades, with swirling banners, with song – who is to say what May Days the future of fate will discover to those who are to come, or what is to grow from the seeds of help or hindrance we sow? All that I know is, now is the time I must tell my story. When the time comes to speak, something within tells me, This one – from across the road, I saw your look through the rain-striped window, and I knew, that this year, this especial year, you are the one I must tell. You are the one who must listen. Whether you will or no.

'There was something mischievous in the man's look, but kindly too, as if he meant, as if he almost said, Hang on.

'The young woman in the apron turned over the cardboard notice that hung crookedly on a string, on the inside of the café door; the word "open" showed on our side, it was closed to the outer world. The Garden Centre would be shut. Anyway, my interest in garden pots had subsided some time ago. I felt – as if I'd been struck a blow on the face, not by a kapo in a camp, but by my own weak and paltry past, my own well-developed and commonplace capacity to deny.

'To make sure it all stayed clear in my mind. I wrote an account of it, as faithfully as I could, on May 1st; the last May Day before the millennium. I had lived my life in a corner of north-east Scotland for some years. I bethought to myself, Mr Julius must be a very old man, very old indeed. He can't go on for ever. Perhaps– just perhaps, I thought,– I might take to travelling about myself for a while. Spring would be a good time of year. That thought led me on, on, the impulse growing to transmit the May Day message. I studied, though that came hard to me. I found books that bore witness, books filled with facts, figures, dates. I learned that what happened is not, to my mind, a subject only for specialist historians. I have learned, learned more than even Mr Julius knew or could tell of, and now my task telling the tale of it is begun.'

My voice falters and stops. I gulp the glass of water. My discarded notes scatter the table. I make to go, stayed by a hand on my arm, applause breaking silence, words of thanks, banging of seat-backs as people grab coats, make for the door; the pale young woman hesitates, her bespectacled friend waits.

SIMON, THINKING THINGS OVER.

Well as sure as my name's Simon, I'd a surprise at that lecture yesterday. Mr Arthur Milne, sixty if he's a day, in the weirdest old pair of trousers, wearing a checked polyester jacket from the year dot – and wanting to call me Mr, until I said, I'm more comfortable being called Simon, let's go for a drink.

He's a man with a permanent buzz. Plants. Latin names and all. What grows where, hairy stems to keep the wind-blown salt off, fleshy leaves, how you take cuttings, ways to spread seeds. Went on worse than our biology teacher used to. An enthusiast.

My grandfather would have liked him. I didn't let on to Arthur how my childhood came to a sudden stop when I overheard grandfather saying something not meant for my ears. Ever after that – the feeling of difference.

Arthur's mind like blotting paper, soaking up information, hooked on new words. Tries to look unselfconscious when he works his new words into the conversation with a sentence he's been composing in his head. Maybe that comes from living on his own all his adult life? I celebrate my own singularity, I even chose a University where Simon's an unusual name – but I must be careful not to become quite as singular as Arthur suggests to me I might.

Being Jewish is a singular feeling although you wouldn't think about it if there wasn't anybody prejudiced against us. That feeling of being special, it's curious, the Germans claimed to be a special race. Historically speaking, can the strands of the thrust towards Fascism in Germany be unravelled, its deepest depths plumbed and fathomed?

Grandfather's ordeal in the concentration camp, mercifully short enough for him to totter out. He'd been wily enough to get by in Berlin for most of the war years, he'd the right sort of knowledge as well as the chance of not looking Jewish. That weird time between the two wars. Grandfather's stories, his beard wagging as he talked; bad times at the end of the 1914 war, near-starvation through the Allied blockade. Crown Prince Willy, as mad in his own way as Hitler in his, reviewing battle-worn-out troops coming back from the front – leaning out of his bedroom window in his pyjamas, a couple of his mistresses on hand. Or seeing a regiment off to be killed in some pointless battle, Willy wearing his tennis flannels and waving his racquet.

In fits and starts my uncle joined in Grandfather's narrative. Duetists, of well-rehearsed themes. The muddled November revolution, soldiers' and workers' soviets springing up everywhere; soldiers holding their guns upside-down to show they were revolutionaries now, but insisting they had to have an officer in charge. Essential to have strong leadership, Uncle's solo predicted; though the Kaiser, who'd wanted to crush the red flag-wavers in Berlin by leading an army against them, came slap-bang against disappointment. Told there was no army, and if there had been it wouldn't have obeyed him. The Kaiser, the Crown Prince too, abdicated, the Kaiser going off to cut down trees in Holland. And oh dear, no Kaiser, no more absolute abasement, came grandfather's caustic commentary. Grandfather reckoned a 'stab-in-the-back' myth got constructed – everything that followed the 1914 war became the fault of the reds and us Jews. I was just a child in years but grandfather didn't go in for dumbing-down.

A naval mutiny saw Lübeck taken over by revolutionaries. Hamburg astir. Officers had their swords confiscated, their shoulder tags cut off – but mostly, with what was considered to be due respect for order. The defeated soldiers kept ranks as they marched back to the Fatherland, before melting away to their homes.

The Rhineland, neat and untouched, Berlin a grim scene. Workers and soldiers, marching together - the Marxist group occupied the Palace, the Social Democrats the Reichstag, a hasty announcement proclaimed a republic; put at the service of a military authority led by Hindenburg. A fatal flaw, said Grandfather shaking his head in distress, Hindenburg was a decayed and greedy old man. But nevertheless, on New Year's Eve 1918, Berliners danced the night away. Deceptions and willed self-deception, commented uncle.

My uncle didn't speak a lot when he first lived with us; but he wrote things down. Perhaps he wanted to explain to us, or even to himself, how on earth it could have happened, in Germany of all places. And Uncle wrote down the story of a con-man who kept up his deception for years, living off the best of everything without paying a penny-piece; revered because of the rumour he'd put about that he was Royalty in disguise. I used to think he'd made the story up, but no, he wasn't imitating Thomas Mann writing Felix Krull the confidence trickster, irony in life can outdo irony in books that ironically foreshadow real events; its humorous course dotted with tragic twists and turns.

After he died I found more papers, scraps written from time to time, I suppose when his mind cleared. Sometimes, like now, I get out the file I assembled, and as I read, it's as if I hear him talking to me:

'Pleasure seeking, the night life of Berlin. That's the image. Who remembers, now, the Freikorps, antecedent of the SS, or the heavy-handed martial law? Who knows of Karl Liebknecht and Rosa Luxemburg other than as names? I could recite for you the bitter details of the arrest of these communists by Freikorps thugs, how they were hit on the head and then, shot. The army's orders on Rosa Luxemburg were most specific; she was not to reach prison alive. After she'd been murdered the official killers threw her body into the canal.'

'A General Strike, called by the Berlin Soviet that Spring. The Freikorps, their brutality unheard of – then. What matter, order was restored, martial law enforced.'

'Bavaria had its own dramas and revolutionary situation. Its own forms of orgiastic madness among its leadership. The Freikorps moved in. The White Terror. Utter brutalities. A group of chimney sweeps shot. Why? The flags that were tokens of their trade, mistaken for the flags of Red Guards. Catholics arrested on suspicion then shot because some army men thought they'd been arrested for their politics. The wall of execution, spattered with blood and brains. These things I saw, forerunners of that which I cannot yet describe.'

And Jane wonders why I wake screaming in the night. I say, it's a nightmare, but I never tell her, not the tales my grandfather told me when I was a little boy. She doesn't know about the accounts my uncle wrote. She doesn't know how when he was caught he saw Günther, the boyhood friend he'd set up in business with a loan from his own struggling shop – before his citizenship had been taken away, of course. Günther's SS uniform, very smart, very correct, a look at Uncle, then away, Uncle hit when he didn't move quickly enough. Which was hard to do, he'd already been beaten up. Uncle's belief in rationality and civilisation, shattered with the mounds of broken window-glass on Kristallnacht. No, I don't tell Jane why I scream aloud in the night, and inside me I scream in the daytime too.

'In 1920, Kapp's soldiery, sprucely turned-out, swastikas on gleaming helmets. The putsch moved them on to the Brandenburger Tor, their entry to Berlin made almost without a struggle. The workers shut down the city with a general strike. On Easter Sunday, truly, on Easter Sunday a massacre at Essen, the Freikorps on the rampage killing whoever they met up with.'

'1923 the great inflation. Our careful middle-class wiped out, the export-business industrialists turning into multi-millionaires almost as fast as the pantomime pumpkin transforms to the gilded coach. 1000,000 mark notes tossed away in the gutter, but fifty dollars would buy you a whole row of the smartest houses in a good street in Berlin.

'How did we stay sane in that kind of climate, where the main requirement of a bank clerk was that he should be good with zeros? Where there was so much crime that prisoners were turned loose from the cells and told to re-apply in due course? Where mass murderers got round the shortage of food by preserving and selling their victims as tasty steaks? Where foreigners on shopping sprees guzzled in Berlin's luxury restaurants and met the bill in their own currency's small change?

'The breakdown of ordinary restraints on sexual behaviour, the whirlwind outbreak of the cabaret scene, the compulsive pleasure-seeking, those strange cults of every variety, involving all ages, all social classes, so long as it was disreputable. Every irrational cult a new fashion for pigs to wallow in. Somebody, I don't recollect his name, even published A Guide to Vicious Berlin.

'The rye mark, that put a stop to inflation. In the last week of November the weekly Berliner Illustreiter Zeitung cost a billion marks. The week after, 30 pfennigs. Not all Germans were pleased, the new currency lost speculators their fortunes -

'As for Hitler's trial after the failure of his Munich putsch, there the accused weren't cross-examined, instead they were indulged and allowed to bully the witnesses. Hitler's defence speech admitted to guilt in the eyes of the law, but insisted on a higher principle of behaviour for himself than law or democratic politics. Then the sentence: four year's fortress arrest, a joke, a form of compliment kept for riotous youth of good family who got involved in a duel, something of that sort. For Hitler, released on probation after only ten months, it represented several steps up the social ladder. And the bright and the dark of Berlin went on as if nothing important had happened, the fast-lane set hectic in their modernity.

'We were an old family, we had lived in Germany since the 12th century. Anti-Semitism became a deepening shadow. Immigrant Jews from Galicia were the strongest opponents of National Socialism. The Christian Churches mouth-shut, religious opposition of a non-political kind yes, from such as Jehovah's Witnesses. In the streets with their propaganda against Hitler but trying also to persuade him they they were not subversives – I can write no more.'

Grandfather, like all us Jews a great talker, a teller of spiced-up tales. As a child I learned the state of his emotions and his mental state, by the waggling of his beard, the extent, the speed, the asymmetry too. Asymmetric waggling was a sign he was seriously put out; if it waggled at speed, that meant he was angry, not angry at me but at the actions of the people he was about to trounce with verbal acid. When he got onto Hindenburg's role, which he frequently did, it waggled alarmingly fast and jerkily.

President Hindenburg, though moribund, had a trick of appearing to be all things to all men, and was especially well thought of by those who approved his complaisance as the Führer-to-be built up a power base. Though Hindenburg had shown as far back as 1925 that he was an enemy of democracy, he was voted in again in 1932. Only a fool could think the 'Old Gentleman' would make a stand for the Constitution. The only consistency of behaviour the old devil had ever shown, said grandfather, was in letting down everyone who'd put their trust in him, the Kaiser, Ludendorf, political leaders: on the right and on the left.

Hindenburg dissolved the Reichstag. There'd been a ban on the SA and the SS, so he lifted it. In the streets violence and murder became a part of life, for some a way of life. Chaos preceded the July elections. A favourite Nazi student chant was, 'We shit on freedom'. And Adolf Hitler presented himself as a unifying force, in a country teetering on the edge of civil war. He still didn't get a voting majority, so he sent for 'the old cab horse', Hindenburg, offered him the post of Chancellor. Hindenburg, a wary old customer, declined.

The National Socialist Party was a clever name, it took in some of the socialists, though most of them believed him not. It had a big and bold appeal to nationalistic sentiments held by the 'little people' who weren't doing at all well, not after the 1929 US slump spread its disastrous effects – my uncle reckoned that if it hadn't been for the first war, the 1914 one, the whole Nazi period, the world war, none of it would have happened. Even after the US loans dried up and wages were low, the highest vote the National Socialists got was eighteen million, with 230 seats in the Reichstag. Then, ber-bump. They lost two million votes and thirtyfour seats. Lost votes in the local elections too. The mood at the time? After the ball was over, I should say might describe it. The Press Ball, the highlight of Berlin's social year, and in 1933 intense nervous excitement together with extreme depression. Would it be Van Papen, vain and incompetent, entering the government box as the new Chancellor, or would it be Hitler? That was the question. That wasn't resolved that night. My uncle had some thoughts about that, on yet another sheet of paper:

'Pressure brought to bear on Hindenburg to ask Hitler to form a government. Hindenburg understood Hitler's intention to rule by dictatorship, so why did he at last agree? The archives give an answer, as archives do – Hindenburg had been given an old family estate by right-wing supporters who saw no point in paying death duties. Some complicated and corrupt deal put the estate in his son Oskar's name. Scandal loomed. Also a putsch might be mounted, if Hitler didn't take over, the Potsdam garrison might topple Hindenburg and put the Army in power. To-and-fro, to-and-fro went the conspirators, throughout that day and the next, before the political office-seekers agreed on Hitler for Chancellor. His first remark to Goebbels as he entered the Chancellery building: 'No one gets me out of here alive'. Small wonder many of us astute Jews decided, time to pack up, leave Germany, get out alive. Yet small wonder many told themselves, we have served in the Germany Army, we can show our war medals, we are well-respected, we will be safe. Your own Grandfather, Simon, determined to stay on in the city he'd always lived in, that had always been home. He wasn't naïve about it, he knew very well what Hitler's intellectual apologist Rosenberg had said, after the trial of five thugs who'd murdered a communist. Rosenberg's comment – bourgeois justice, mirroring the ideology of the past 150 years, values the life of a single communist, a Pole at that, against five German war veterans, which was unacceptable to the world view of National Socialism, which does not believe one man is equal to another, does not believe in rights as such, it aims to create the German man of strength. And for good measure Rosenberg added that all justice, all social life, politics and economics must be subordinated to the task of protecting the German Republic.'

Hitler in power. The first concentration camps, set up straight away, instruments of State terror to suppress resistance and prepare for all-out war. Just like that wary old bird Thomas Mann reckoned. The Nazis made bonfires of his books. But it was worse for Walter Benjamin. His most precious thing in life was his collection of books, twice burned; once in Germany, then after he'd fled to France and started over, again the Nazis came. He'd tried to get to Spain across the mountain pass by the goat tracks over the Pyranees, refugees did that all the time, up an established passportless refugee route. He'd tried it on the one night peoples' papers were checked. It was random bad luck he got turned back; but he couldn't face making that climb again. Grandfather's beard signalled to me his own distress at that true story.

Once, Jane said to me, 'Why don't you grow a beard? I felt her hurt, as I abruptly pulled away from her. I never try to explain. Sometimes I think we hardly know each other. That time we had a row.... I didn't hit her, I think she thought I might ....

Walter Benjamin. Dead from a self-inflicted bullet. Only one more tragic loss of a life? Shouldn't each and everyone of the lost ones have someone to acknowledge our loss of their talent, remember their pain? My Uncle would have thought so, unable to speak when they carried him out of the camp on a stretcher.

ARTHUR AWAKES

What woke me? For heaven's sake, what? I'm, where, yes home in bed. Safe. Safe safe safe. Sad. No, not sad. I've had a fright, that's all – that dream. Did I? I suppose I must have. Can't even remember what the beastly dream was about. Oh yuk. Mouth furred, beastly head – truly hungover.

Sisyphus. It was about Sisyphus. The chap in that old Greek story. Don't remember what he got up to to get his punishment, annoyed the Gods I suppose. Disobeyed. Had to roll a great huge stone up the hill. Nearly to the top, he couldn't get it up the last steepnesses of the slope, sweat and strain, every last effort no use, it rolls back on him, going down, gaining momentum it gaining speed him gaining despair as it goes rolling down down. To the bottom of the hill. Start all over again, sorry sirs, let me appease your anger. Let me off, I won't do it again. And the Gods? Roaring with laughter, were they? Falling about pissing themselves with the humour of it, jolly good show chaps, we know he can't get it to the top don't we.

Me. A bit of the Sisyphus about me, these days? Yesterday – well, I didn't get anywhere near the top yesterday. When I picked my dratted notes up I came to my senses, I'd scarcely told them anything about the resistance groups in the camps. Rant rant rant, like Mr Julius did when he got worked up, that wasn't how I'd meant to do it – quiet, serious, names and dates, that's how it was intended to be. After all, they were academics, never had that level of education myself, doesn't mean I don't respect it or know it's statistics and stuff like that, that's needed to convince them.

Well. Turn again, Whittington. Time to get up. Or, five minutes more? If I'd still been at work, I wouldn't have the choice. Nor I wouldn't if... Now stop it Arthur, just you stop it, no use to go down that old worn-out track. What happened, happened. You're not even a market-gardener any more. Much less the landscape gardener you'd thought you'd found your chance with.

Not that it was my fault that boom went bust, just when I'd got the bank loan to fund the business, and the interest rate went up to 15%. I hung on too long, yes, but how could I just chuck the towel in – you shut your eyes to the interest mounting up, interest on interest, unbelievable really. Bin the monthly bank statement, hope for the best. Perhaps Sisyphus was a hoper-for-the-best too?

Repossession's a funny word when you think about it. Like redundant. They hadn't thought up down-sizing then. Reparations, another troublesome word. Then there's relocation. I relocated to a bungalow. Well I call it a bungalow so nobody feels sorry for me living in a run-down old place, after what I'd had. It's the tiny garden that bothers me, padded out with garden pots of all things – but at least I've got somewhere to sit out. And I cleared off every last penny of debt. Some satisfaction to that, like seeing a garden cleared of weeds.

Afterwards it all seems – thin. You look at the plans, an old garden you've re-created, the knot beds, the statues spouting out water into the shining pool with a fountain in the middle, the ... oh, hell, you can't smell the flowers anymore, you don't see it, not really see it alive and growing, and it's a funny thing but the taste of everything is – just cardboard. Life, a flat surface, nothing behind it. What a joke, it's the latest fad these days, they're at the lost gardens thing on the telly, no blisters on their hands that I've noticed.

That's over, chucked away. In another lifetime. Put another record on. On the nickelodeon. Closer, my dear come closer. Cheap rubbish, that. And I got scared, not knowing what I might be getting into. Uncharted waters, not for me. Or so I thought.

Why don't I put my mind to it, the Ode to Joy, Sing, in the German then. If I can: 'Wir sind die Moorsoldaten, und spehen' – is it 'spehen'? mit dem spaten' – I'm sure it's 'spaten' when they went out to dig the peat, it was blisters, aching backs, sore feet and empty bellies too, I shouldn't wonder – and there's that other one, the marching one from Sachsenhausen, 'Help in word and help in deed, every comrade who's in need', well even if it sounds corny, sententious, aren't we all in need in one way or another?

Relocation. From a bad place to a worse. From the ghetto where the food allowance was set so you only three-quarters starved, marched to a camp. If you were lucky – ha-ha – a slaveworkers' camp. If not so lucky, shunted straight to a death camp. Sobibor, Treblinka, Belzec.

Evacuation. That meant you were going to be killed, finished off before you got the chance to be liberated. It's nice when you can kid yourself there's going to be a happy ending.

I still miss him, Angus, my dear and only brother, an older brother part of childhood and growing up, not ever out of my deepest thoughts. That last trip to sea… where strange things happen. I used to be sick as a dog when the wind got up. Terrified. The old-time fishermen believed the sea took men for its revenge on the takers of its fish.

He loved the sea, did Angus. Onshore, he was always wanting to be away again. Said he'd rather be out there in the lash of the rain than reading about it in somebody's old poem.

Funny thing about that Ancient Mariner piece. Not a word in it, about why the wretched bird got shot. One minute the crew were all over it, what a lovely bird, this albatross is come to play and lark about with us whenever we call it – and next thing off, it's, 'With my crossbow I shot the albatross.' So, an accident, did the mariner take against it, think it'd make a tasty supper, or what? Did the skipper give him an order, shoot that blasted noisy bird? We don't get to find out. But the crew all go along with it, they get struck dead for blaming the bird for bringing them the bad weather. Just as if they'd got their armbands on. Then all that stuff with the mariner, with the bird he can't get from round his neck, and the thirst, the piercing thirst, like the thirst of the helpless, old and young, children, babies even, packed into truckloads on the trains to Auschwitz, and the so-efficient Germans wouldn't provide so much as a drop of water for the journey, the mariner thirsting, his own fault though, to the moment of his seeing the beauty of the sea creatures he'd been cursing. A discovery of …

If I hadn't had my place repossessed: would I have had the ghost of an idea of what it felt like for ordinary German blokes, chaps not unlike me, when that Adolph and his lot started speechifying? Worse there than the thirties depression here, of course. Worse than in America, though they had their rocky years too, with soup kitchens and breadlines and not far off from having a revolution, though that's hard to believe when you look at how they got going after the War, how they make the money these days. Stock market fortunes. Bit of a difference from the time Bing Crosby used to croon, 'Once I built a railroad, now it's done, Buddy, can you spare a dime.' Only a kid myself, but I remember the harsh times.

War reparations. Inflation, another of those dried-out evaporated terms economists use, cool, galloping inflation, who did the galloping, to my mind it was the workers, paid twice a day, who galloped out to spend their money, it'd not be worth much if they stopped to count it. Seven million men and women chucked on the scrap heap, no work no money not much of anything but misery for anyone who was pensioned off to waste away on.

Simon said his grandfather told him a lot, if I didn't believe it I could read it for myself. Books, books and music. Theatres, cinemas, come to the cabaret. The Germans known for it. I didn't like to ask Simon what he meant by 'blood and soil' writers, and overblown romanticism nonsense. Am I going out of my mind? No. I don't think so. I'm upset after yesterday, I'd meant to be so precise. Oh my head. Coffee. Damn, I've dropped the jar. Doesn't spread so far as broken eggs, though. And. And. Even if the bloody rock keeps slipping down again, I will, I will try to keep pushing the bugger back up. There, most of the spilled stuff's up now. Like Simon said, I could write down what I've learned about the camps' resistance movements, the rebellions, dignity maintained. Like Simon insisted.

There's so much not known, so much that can't be known. Lorry-loads where no-one survived to tell the tale of what they'd done or tried to do. Shouts someone heard. Shots. Gypsies who knew they were being taken away to die, who put up a fight first. – I felt quite a shiver, reading about the letter Z. Z for Zigeuner. A song about a gypsy playing a tune on the violin – 'Play for me, Zigeuner', sounds so romantic, the gypsy a tall man with a glossy moustache, a coloured scarf wound tight round his head and a smirk on his face as he helps the seduction scene along with gooey music. That's how I'd thought of Zigeuner until I realised that in the Nazi State a Gypsy wasn't allowed a country of his own, just the letter Z. A little child who survived remembered an Auschwitz song of theirs – asking a blackbird to fly away with a message, to tell everybody about the smoke from the chimneys.

I told Simon in the pub last night, it'd be a lot easier for him to write it all down than for me – good job I caught the last bus home. Decent of the driver to pull up, wait while Simon shoved me up the steps, me trying to find my return ticket. I daresay I made a right fool of myself. Didn't throw up, though, not so far as I can remember. A long time since I got as drunk as that, as blind drunk as mind drunk as drunk as a skunk drunk. I hope I haven't lost his address, fancy his grandfather and his uncle both being ... No wonder he wanted to know if I was qualified to speak about it. My head! Water, that's the thing. God, is that my tongue looking like an old doormat? Arthur, Arthur, for shame. Ah! here's the name, Simon Goldberg, and the address, Old Aberdeen near the University. His girlfriend, Jane.

There were warning signs. 1930. The September elections rang alarm bells. That writer, Thomas Mann, not read him myself, heavy going I should think, but credit to him, he tried to put people on their guard, though he bit off more than he could chew, at that big meeting in Berlin that Simon told me about. Mann was a famous writer, he thought they'd listen to him if he turned up and spoke out.

Some hopes. Nazi youths all over the hall yelled him down. Mann's Jewish friend Bruno Walter, who'd conducted concerts by the dozen in Berlin, got him out, he knew the connecting corridors through to the Philharmonic Hall next door. I can just see them, groping their way along in the dark, until at last, Hurray, there's the Kathenerstrasser exit. Where Bruno Walter had parked his car. Perhaps he'd more idea than Mann of how far hysteria had already got in its take-over from reason.

Hitler had a daft plan to emigrate the Jews, all, to Madagascar, so he said. Pre-war, some could buy their way out. Some stayed on, getting by in a twilight world of forged passports, black marketing for food; helped, hidden, betrayed, ignored by turns. Simon's grandfather, riding on a Berlin tram, relying on his Aryan looks. Not far off, a mother with her little girl. A shabby woman, timidly silent, keeping her head down, not meeting anyone's eye. Her child, neatly dressed. The yellow Star of David on each of their coats, people in the tram keeping away from them. The child's huge eyes. A woman in a warm coat, who fumbles in her bag. Who gets up from her seat. Who bustles her way to the little girl, hands the child – a little paper bag. The child clutches it, the woman goes back to her seat, uncomfortable silence fills the trying-not-to-look, not-to-see tramload. There's the rustle of paper as the child opens the bag. She finds sweets. She pulls one out, a bright red one. She stares at it eyes wide, before putting it, very solemnly, into her mouth, and sucking it. I daresay the sweet was slightly sticky. The child licks her fingers, despite her mother's embarrassed attempt to urge polite restraint – she doesn't have the luxury of a handkerchief, I suppose.

The German woman's action. Reasons unfathomable. Consequences unknown. Sometimes I walk on stretches of sandy shore, thinking of consequences you mightn't expect. Tide rolls in, the wind off the sea blows sand way back to cover the shore road, it leaves a flat bared spread of beach. Lichen, mosses, then tiny plants get a foothold, a build-up into little hillocks begins. Marram grass turns up from wherever, it adapts to the salt, the dry cutting wind, its roots cling, its tall stems bend to the force from the sea, sand dunes form, roots spread deep and wide, gripping, holding the sand together, and the shore life, insects and birds and the flowering lichens, mosses and heathers accumulate. There's a lot of things learn to grow, even in sand. Root systems spread out, oh, yards, I should say, under the ground.

Underground. I read about the ghetto in Cracow, after Poland was invaded; ways to get in or out through the sewers, if you knew the way and were desperate enough to tackle the danger, the horror of that route, the risks – knowing if you're spotted climbing out you'll be shot in the back of the neck, that's if you're lucky enough to get such an easy way to get your toes turned up.

Lists of names. 'Pack your cases, you're going to a work camp.' The Jews were careful people, they painted their names on the suitcases that held their clothes, their useful things, their family photographs. Rumours, spreading through the ghetto. Work-camps where ghetto-dwellers were despatched by train – not big enough, not by a long chalk, for all those sent there; who didn't come out. Trains arriving back from Treblinka had loads of human hair. The Polish Home Army managed to get samples for analysis. And found – hydrogen cyanide. So the Jews still in the Ghetto decided. The Home Army supplied guns and ammunition. More guns, some bought from German sources. The first skirmish, January 1943. In April German artillery and incendiary bombs overwhelmed resistors' rifles and home-made grenades. Systematic annihilation to follow. But a hundred or so Germans were killed, war factories destroyed. About a hundred Jews escaped through the sewers. It took until the end of May for the Nazis to empty the ghetto. Four hundred thousand souls, either there or in the camps, who didn't survive.

All part of the plan. Goebbels kept a diary, there's an entry in it for the 27th March

1942. The usual wording, the Jews to be 'relocated' using, 'a fairly basic procedure, one that cannot be precisely described', 60% to be liquidated, 40% sent to labour detachments. The ghettos to be emptied, filled again with a new consignment deported from the Reich, these moved on, until 'not many of the Jews will be left over.' The fulfilment of Hitler's mad prophecy, the very core of the Nazi world view. Chelmno, Belzec, Treblinka, Sobibor, its dedicated death sites.

JANE THINKS

Simon was a bit hard on Arthur, I thought. Simon can be sharp, I know. When we first got together, I did wonder if it would work. He simply can't resist arguing. That's the Jewish heritage. Questioning everything, turning and twisting ideas every which way. Yet Arthur didn't mind. We got on well when we ended up at the pub. Arthur surprising. Couldn't spot his accent. Old-fashioned vocabulary. Dowdily dressed in old clothes. Then his childhood, north-east Scotland; working in England, learning to speak in a way they accepted.

Knowing where someone's started from. That's a help. Usually. Couldn't help laughing as the drinking got going. Stopped laughing though, when they got onto Hitler. Simon of course told his stories about Bruno Walter, in March 1933 after Hitler got to power. Walter's brilliant success in New York. His astonishment, coming back to Germany, swastika flags in the streets, cautious looks, the anxious look already dubbed the 'Neue Deutsche Rundschau'. Arthur looked so blank at that point, Simon told him, it was black humour, it meant, the New German Survey.

The Leipzig Nazis prevented Bruno Walter's concert there. The Gewandhaus management committee refused his offer to resign, relying on their proud traditions, and even hoping Winifred Wagner would intercede, use her influence with Goering and her friend Herr Hitler. Some hopes, hadn't she supplied Hitler with the paper to write 'Mein Kampf' on, while he was in jail?

In Berlin, his concert wasn't banned. Just his contract cancelled, when Dr. Funk informed the management, if they insisted on going ahead, they could be certain sure that everything in the hall would be smashed to smithereens. You couldn't blame the management for calling it off, considering what did happen in Berlin. Dozens of Storm Troopers burst in to the Mozartsaal cinema, Goebbels with them, shouting insults, letting off stink bombs, throwing bags of sneezing powder, letting mice out. Remarque's anti-war film All Quiet on the Western Front was showing.

Bruno Walter went, like quite a few others, to Austria. He was working in Amsterdam when Austria was invaded; it was his daughter, who'd stayed at home, who got arrested. And even Furtwängler, who'd been well in as a conductor for Hitler, got pulled up short, lost all his prestigious posts, though he crawled to Goebbels, after he wrote an article in praise of Hindemith's banned music and for artistic freedom.

Simon's advice to Arthur, very emphatic, when he read his notes. Too much, much too much, Arthur, even for a whole series of lectures. And these days, we students want courses to help us on with our careers. Future financial wizardry, fireworks to rocket us up to electronic fortunes, milli-billy-onaires, Simon says. Stand up, hands up, hands on heads, do what entrepreneurs have to do. Well, what else is there for us to do, these days, we missed out on a whale of a time in the sixties, got bogged down, didn't we, in all the Thatcher years?

This coffee's foul. Was Simon right, telling Arthur to write a book about the resistance? Such a strange thing Arthur said, when he told us how he'd felt when his landscape-gardening business failed; that phrase he'd used, how it had been dreich November even in May, and the haar misted over everything like a window that wanted cleaning. Not good years for him. Meeting Mr Julius stopped him faffing around. Simon says, there's a strenuous happiness when the task is difficult but necessary. I can't find the task.

Simon took it on himself to educate Arthur on the National Socialist Party.Question: What did they do on gaining power? Answer: Outlawed the Communist Party, seized its property, hunted down its members. Next came the Social Democratic Party, its meetings banned, its newspapers closed down. Next, the Nationalists.

The Catholic Centre didn't wait to be banned, it closed itself down. As did the Bavarian People's Party. Hey presto, first it's a democracy, then it's not, every political party except the National Socialists blown away. The Trades Unions banned. Every democratic institution eliminated one by one, by 14th July Hitler's party becomes the State itself. Neat as the three card trick.

Simon researched the evidence for an underground movement in Germany. Industriously put it together. He's told me, more than once, the way publications with innocent-sounding titles somehow appeared – a desperately serious topic, so when Simon's uncle first told him and me about those pamphlets it was awful of me to spot a weird resemblance to the song Don Juan's servant Leporello sings in Mozart's 'Don Giovanni', when he's listing all the Don's conquests, so many in each country, the list goes on and on. Simon's Uncle wrote down the list: forty-eight pamphlets on general anti-Nazi themes, twelve containing anti-war propaganda, eighteen worker's pamphlets, four more produced by intellectuals, five by Catholics, four against the persecution of the Jews, five that make an appeal to youth, twenty-five which give explanations of communism, fifteen about aspects of life in the Soviet Union. Another nineteen periodicals – but as the uncle sadly said, most of those ended, the last one known of dated 1942. Refugees in exile, who put out information and exhortation from afar. Scattered groups in Germany. Jehovah's Witnesses, who wouldn't say 'Heil Hitler' or raise an arm in a Nazi salute, printing their 'Watchtower' on secret presses, miniature Bibles to smuggle in to their brothers and sisters, held in prisons since 1929 then sent to camps – even a specially made gramophone playing a suitably Witness message.

Simon's grandfather, gone underground, dodging informers but rounded up at last, surviving the camp on his belief that it was his sort who represented all that was best in the Fatherland's way of life. One simple sustaining idea. He might die, yes, but he wouldn't die degraded, he wouldn't snatch at survival like a wounded beast. The 'politicals' with their sustaining idea, the religiously motivated with their own equally powerful determination to remain staunch – the Jehovah's only had to sign the statement regularly put in front of them, renouncing their beliefs and kow-towing to Hitler, to be released. They prayed instead, not to get out but to endure all they must endure with continuing staunchness. And helped each other sharing bits of bread.

Hearing Simon go on about the underground publications must have stamped that list into my memory circuits. The uncle's claim, when he began to talk again, agonised fragments, at first in writing – he was glad to be fully conscious again, which nobody believed he would be when he was liberated. His claim that those publications are the visible sign of underground opposition, changing form as the situation changed, continuing the base for communicating with the imprisoned – strengthening their resistance when, discovered, their authors were arrested and imprisoned in their turn. Law is what I've chosen to study, not history. I might, though, I might look up more of that stuff on the Nuremberg trials.

ARTHUR – AGAIN

I still see them, children wearing the striped uniforms. One little one, buttons done up lopsided, a coat on underneath. A boy in the front row pushes up his left sleeve, holds it back, holds up his arm so the cameraman can get a clear shot of the tattooed letter and number on the inner side of his forearm. Is the boy stoical, or accusing? Another lad, older, dark-eyed, has a strange look about him, Charlie Chaplin as a starving young kid. A woman, maybe a nurse, holds a sick child in her arms. On each side, wire fences. I hope the electricity supply's been turned off, awful to have accidental deaths just before they begin to think of themselves as ex-prisoners.

If you got tattooed, that meant you'd been passed fit for work; not allocated for medical experiments, not for the gas chamber either, not until your strength gave out.

The wisdom of the child. Would it be so unreasonable for him, arguing from experience, to show off the tattoo, regarded as his personal triumph within the camp system, rather than as an outsider view of it as the sign of humiliation deliberately imposed? I've pondered for hours on hours, brooding over that child's face, his look straight at me, I can't fathom what it is he wants me to know.

There's something about him that raised a memory. That photograph, and the other photograph. Children saved from Auschwitz, looking at the camera's lens is picture number one. Picture number two, from the United States of America. A group of boys, wearing caps, faces grimed, staring at the camera's lens, with such eyes; an old photograph, from the time, early nineteenth century, when mine-workers' children had to work at sorting the coal that came up along the conveyor belts, stones and slate to be got out by those boys, yes their eyes accused with bitter looks, not childlike – just their looks to speak for them. Now those two photographs merge in my mind. Damnation.

Someone must have given them food, you can see that, as they stand stock still near the exit gate, not knowing what's going to happen next, where they'll be taken to or any of that. But they know it won't be to the gas chambers, you have to form up in lines of five for that. They stare at the camera, as if to say look, we are the only ones left alive. I can't make out what's behind their eyes, they have seen things that are beyond me. So did Jewish children who were hidden away with Christian foster-parents, taught their new names, taught by nuns in convents how to cross themselves, taught by partisans to lie low in forest hideouts, taught to be silent when their parents pushed them into a tiny cupboard space when a knock came on the door, taught to insist to the SS questioners that no, they were not Jewish, false names false family names false histories rolling from their childish tongues that must say, no, there is no-one hidden in the attic, taught to endure the dark and stink of the Warsaw sewers months on end, taught to be hungry, taught to stay on the move, not draw attention to themselves by saying anything clever, learning through betrayals and unselfish help alike that their childhood was over, gone, unretrievable. And despite all that some who survived managed to retrieve in their adult lives the sense of what they could do to be rescuers of traumatised others.

Come on, Arthur, begin it at the beginning –

DACHAU

The first concentration camp, Dachau, was set up in 1933 near a derelict explosives factory. The first 2,000 prisoners slept in abandoned concrete huts; the features common to all such camps – barbed wire, electrified fences, watchtowers, were devised at Dachau. By 1937, Dachau prisoners including political dissidents, Jews and a contingent of Jehovah's Witnesses – one hundred and fifty had been sent there in 1936 from various prisons – were used to build a new camp, barracks with tiers of wooden bunks for prisoners and comfortable quarters for the SS. Kitchens, workshops, showers, an infirmary. Punishment cells, nicknamed 'the bunkers'. A crematorium. A Commandant was required; Höss, who later became notorious at Auschwitz, learned his trade at Dachau, being replaced on September 1st 1942, when prisoners' work became more important to the regime than their swift extinction. The new commandant, Martin Weiss, is said by the camp's chronicler-prisoners, Arthur Haulot and Ali Kuci, to have improved living conditions to such an extent that they became almost bearable. And Dachau enlarged, swollen with at least 130 subsidiary camps and fifteen for women prisoners. This expansion gave greater opportunities for resistance to those who did not accept the 'Führer' principle of command and obey. Included amongst these were the Jehovah's Witnesses transferred there from Gestapo prisons, helped to survive by their community-oriented attitudes.

Similarly, when Viennese Jews arrived at Dachau after Kristallnacht in November 1938, not yet automatically stripped of all valuable possessions, some had jewels, or money. They could buy things from the prisoners' canteen. Others among them were very poor. And the rich Jews, as a German put in charge of a block of prisoners noted, set up a communal kitty. They paid money in, the poor Jews took money from it as needed. Until the camp administration found out, confiscated the kitties and punished all the block personnel for letting such an un-Nazi thing happen.

Gestapo rules for breaking people's spirit were circumvented in other ways, for instance by listening to broadcasts from foreign radio stations – radios were constructed in one of the workshops, and listened to from the Spring of 1939, in the seclusion of a room in a safe part of the laundry. One radio was hidden in a watering can, another concealed in Block 20. Specialists used their skills to make and repair these secret radios, diverting parts salvaged from shot-down aircraft.

After that first, and probably worst, commandant had been replaced, those of the resistance who gained office jobs seized opportunities to transfer reliable men to subsidiary camps, where they sought to make contact with local people, give them information on the camps and spread radio-gathered news on the worsening war situation.

Austrians were well represented, especially after the transfer of a group of several hundred Austrian ex-Spanish civil war fighters in 1941, on May 1st. Later that year, great numbers of Russian prisoners-of-war were taken – killed before they reached the camp, their uniforms arrived for disinfection, revealing their fate. They would be followed by living captured soldiers in 1942.

On May 9th 1942 the administration had decided the crematoria facilities were inadequate. New and improved versions called Barracks X were designed, to be built, as usual, by prisoners; and in this case by a work detail led by the German communist Karl Wagner, a mason by trade. He gave clear, detailed instructions to the men working for him. Addressing them as comrades, he urged on them the necessity of ensuring this murderous assignment would not be completed. Not only slow working, he told them, but sabotage was the thing, wherever it could be managed.

Following on this injunction, foundations turned out to be too weak, and cement would not set properly. Mortar crumbled between the bricks. Whole units had to be pulled down and re-erected. After a string of such delays, the crematorium did at last get finished – but by that time the situation had changed; as events moved on, the SS lost interest in the gas chambers. Wagner's ingenuity as well as the modest courage he showed in this stalling and balking of SS intentions, is an example of an effective retort to Nazi power by the ragged, the shoeless underdogs.

Organisers of sabotage also made creative use of the SS card-index system which listed inmates' work skills. Prisoners gained jobs as clerks in the Work Assignment Office, then re-classified unskilled workers as experts and assigned them to skilled work in arms factories. There quick-witted opportunists such as an Austrian veteran of the Spanish civil war, Heribert Kreutzmann, used his initiative to misplace screws and other production parts in a war factory; his misdeeds were discovered, but friends got him sent to Auschwitz as a nurse, evading the death sentence that automatically followed the discovery of sabotage.

Nor were women deterred. An experimental project using women workers to make rubber from a plant source somehow did not produce any useful results; and a Polish woman, Matilda Brozek, is known to have damaged machinery in a cartridge factory (with the approval of the German foremen, who shielded her when she was betrayed); she too was protectively moved to another camp.

By 1942 surviving Soviet officers began to make links with German and Austrian representatives of the camp committees. In another development that autumn the Dachau organisation sent Karl Wagner to a small camp in the Tyrol area, to work as a construction foreman. With him were eight tried and tested veterans of the International Brigade. Among their set tasks, they were instructed to make contact with partisans known to be fighting in the Tyrolean mountains.

Such steadfastness had many outcomes. Block 9 had become the quarantine quarters for prisoners afflicted with scabies, a horribly itchy, highly infectious skin condition. When rations for this block were cut to bread alone, Hugo Guttman, the senior block inmate, together with all the block personnel, amazed the officer-in-charge by asking to be relieved of their duties, since they could not bear to watch any more deaths – they would rather be locked up in the punishment cells themselves than look on while people starved to death. Following this protest, rations for the block were restored to the usual level.

For sheer audacity, the theatrical performances – the theatre being so close and dear to German culture – that followed from permission to put on shows, is a hard act to follow. The first play was put on at Christmastime 1941. The Nazis attended all performances, so the pointed satire in the one-act plays devised by Johann Nepomuk Nestroy was a skating on the thinnest of thin ice. The Austrian journalist Rudolf Kalmar remarked how far he went in the ambiguously named farce, 'The Bloody Night on the Schreckenstein, or, That is Not True Love'. In this the protagonist resembled Hitler; the political allusions brought roars of laughter from the prisoners. The SS were either too thick to get the point or found it impossible to credit what their ears were hearing.

The Social Democratic prisoners did not have the wealth of experience acquired by the communists in the course of their years of conspiratorial activity – Schorch Scherer, a German communist, had been at Dachau since 1935, becoming its first senior camp inmate – and were, overall, fewer in number and older in age; their active interest in camp affairs had its great positive effects in the infirmary. French and Czech prisoners had the greatest numbers of medical doctors amongst them; at Dachau the name of Fratislek Braha became known as one who helped many patients to survive. The technique of name swapping developed during the time Albert Guérisse (that was his camp name, he was really an O'Leary) worked in the infirmary. Learning that the SS intended to kill a Russian, he substituted the number of a Pole who had just died. The trick worked; afterwards those working as nurses kept a sharp lookout for opportunities to repeat the swapping the numbers of endangered prisoners with the names and numbers of those who had already passed beyond the reach of the SS.

The file clerks devised methods to save lives. For instance, Joseph Rovan noted the name of a Dutch captain who was listed for 'special treatment' on arrival at the camp – in the coded SS terminology, execution. When the Gestapo delivered him at the camp, Rovan hid his file card. Every time the Dutchman was looked for, it was said he still hadn't arrived, no, no file card, not present, couldn't be found; he remained successfully hidden in one of the barracks.

There were clergymen of all denominations sent to camps because they opposed the system, and given a hard time of it; all known ones were sent to Dachau. Himmler, rabidly homophobic, had convinced himself that Catholic priests menaced the continuation of the German 'race' by practising and spreading homosexual behaviour. Nonetheless they managed to smuggle out news, and succeeded in having a so-called euthanasia project stopped – after that, clergymen could not be used for medical experiments. Keeping their faith became for the assorted clergymen an act of inner resistance; despite official policy, a deacon had the last rites administered to him.

The Nazis in charge of camp policy were obsessively keen to brutalise their prisoners, setting them against each other in every way they could devise. During 1942, an order commanded that the routine beatings for minor infringements of a rule would in future be carried out, not by the guards, but by the prisoners themselves. Many instances show this was resisted, both in the main camp and in its subsidiary camp Allach, where conditions were dire. The veteran prisoner Walter Wagner arranged with the camp committee, that he should be sent to Allach to improve things. There, appointed senior camp inmate, he was the first to refuse to whip Russian, Polish and Yugoslav fellow prisoners, boldly stating that he didn't give beatings. Taken to the bunker in Dachau, in the punishment cell, discharged from his privileged position, he was punished with twenty-five blows – then re-instated. Other names of honour for a like refusal are, Hans Biederer, three teeth knocked out on the spot, a whipping, then locked up, and transfer to another camp. Kaspar Bachl, much the same treatment; also Karl Frey. (Of Frey's behaviour it has been said, by Leopold Arthofer, that his glory lives on in the grateful hearts of a thousand former camp inmates.) A senior block inmate in the main camp, an Austrian communist called Hans Vetrofsky, also carried out his party's decision to refuse to obey the order to beat someone up. He was whipped for it, but retained his armband.

When Edmont Michelet, a French Catholic, was sent to Dachau in 1943, the German and Austrian Catholics got him a position in the disinfection detail, where he helped the large numbers of Frenchmen – mostly politicals – who arrived from June 1944 onwards. Later that year a link-up took place between the French and the other groups, creating an inclusive inter-national organisation whose members agreed to differ on their various political approaches.

Escaping was particularly difficult before 1943. At a subsidiary camp near Hallein, Sepp Plieseis met up with comrades who helped him escape. Not to be outdone his friend Leo Jansa also succeeded, though not until the end of 1944. Though few, successful escapes showed that the Nazis could be outwitted.

But there were setbacks for the organisation too. A hundred or so communist resisters, their names betrayed to the camp management by informers, were sent off to other camps, weakening the organisation. An SS investigation and report had shown they suspected a Communist conspiracy, by German and Austrian political prisoners who after ten or more years of detention had still not been ground down, whose acts of sabotage, their solidarity and friendship shown to 'foreigners', challenged the 'law and order' of the camp.

News from the outer world, however risky to obtain, became vitally important as changes in the war situation raised hopes of freedom. In the SS quarters at Dachau, in the SS canteen, radio listening led to the news of the Allied landing in Normandy being passed around the camp by 9am on the selfsame morning the tale of it was broadcast.

The problems of staying alive multiplied as many thousands of prisoners from sites closer to the front line began to be dumped at the already overcrowded camp. Increasing chaos and deprivation were followed by an outbreak of typhus, chronic undernourishment, then outright famine. The Buchenwald people were among those arriving. One trainload on the tracks outside the camp could not be unloaded for lack of space. When at last the trucks were unsealed most of the people in them were already dead from hunger, thirst, the heat in the sealed cars. The resistance groups decided that some form of action, however risky, must be undertaken.

The 1,400 SS men over them were armed with guns, explosives and poison gas – and rabid hatred made more dangerous by their growing fear. Of the 35,000 prisoners, half were ill, all were weakened by malnutrition. Their leaders had been transported away to other camps. Many of the remaining Germans were 'greens', ready to side with the camp management. Nevertheless the recently-appointed senior camp inmate, Oskar Müller, and the Belgian Arthur Haulot, got in touch with each of the committees, forming groups that would take steps to protect people in the camps, in the dangerous gap between the expected collapse of the system and the arrival of the liberating armies. Any attempt at a breakout would, they knew, result in huge casualties, so a fall-back plan for open revolt would only be used if the SS began a massacre.

April 23rd 1945 saw 2,400 weak and emaciated Jews rounded up, the first act of an order to evacuate all Jews, 'without exception'. During that night the camp resistance sought to co-ordinate its planned actions, based on information from radio news bulletins, information on SS movements, and the situation within the camp itself. The camp commandant was losing control, of himself as well as the camp. The SS were hard at it, destroying all compromising documents – aided by prisoners who took the golden opportunity to burn lists of prisoners, while especially wanted prisoners of various nationalities were hidden, mostly in the hospital block.

The famine increased, the typhus outbreak was spreading; with two hundred deaths each day, scenes in the hospital were like scenes from hell. An air-raid warning lasted all night. Next morning it sounded again, but all were glad, for so long as the raid lasted there would not be another evacuation procedure. Documents had been found, including an order signed by Himmler, which stated that the surrender of the camp was absolutely out of the question, the camp must be evacuated immediately. The document ended with the terrible statement, 'No prisoner must be allowed to fall into the hands of the enemy alive.'

Jews loaded on wagons on the 24th were still there. 700 of them had already died. Then an order came on the 26th; at twelve o'clock everyone had to be formed up in the roll call area ready to march. The resistance organisation abandoned hope for the survival of its own members, resolving to do all they could for the 77,000 souls still in Dachau and its satellite camps, by causing chaos and delay to thwart the evacuation.

By this time some of the SS were cringing. Messages arriving from the central administration were soon known about by the prisoners. At the satellite camp of Landsberg, a guard had opened the gate for four men, letting them out in exchange for a tin of meat. A prisoner detail and two guards walked out, determined to find American forces. Karl Reimer also made up his mind to escape, for the same purpose. Civilian clothes were available in the camp, from a recent transport there of people from Natzweiler. Riemer and others of the same mind fitted themselves out with civilian clothes. Together with an SS man who wanted to do a bunk, seventeen prisoners were escorted out by the guard.

Outside the camp, they were forced to split up, to evade all sorts of danger. The enterprising Riemer reached a liberated town, Pfaffenhofen, but not until the 29th, at about midday. Riemer got to see an American commander, stressing that the situation at Dachau was critical, not a moment should be lost in coming to their aid. The commander promised to help them.

At the camp evacuation remained the main threat. A contingent should have been lined up for evacuation at 12 o'clock. By 2pm the line-up could be no longer delayed, but then the commandant was persuaded by Felix Maurer, who brought him coffee, to rescind the order. The commandant left in a panic-stricken state. Unfortunately the officer-in-charge did not carry out the order, with the result that 7,000 or 8,100 had to march off - the great majority of them walking skeletons.

The next group scheduled to go did benefit from the deliberate delays. An air raid warning sounded repeatedly from 10.30 am, while the rumble of artillery announced the imminent arrival of Allied troops. At this crucial time the resistance did not know that Riemer had achieved his SOS on their behalf. Some escaped and found shelter in the town of Dachau. There Walter Neff and Geog Scherer and his family (both these men were discharged prisoners from Dachau who had kept in contact) provided them with civilian clothes, food and shelter.

On April 28th the radio station repeatedly broadcast a statement from a group calling itself 'Bavarian Freedom Action'. This appeal, made by the Freedom Action group, sparked an immediate response. Citizens of Dachau and escapees from the camp rushed the Town Hall and occupied it. SS units attacked them; three men from the camp, a German and two Austrian veterans of the Spanish civil war, were among those who were killed. But not uselessly, for after this the SS guards decided their time was up and left. So it was that this joint action formed part of the overall strategy of stopping more evacuations. Indeed, by the later stages, some of the younger SS men appeared to be on the prisoners' side, passing information on to them and helping them in active opposition work. When women prisoners were brought in, guarded by women in SS uniforms, these SS women actually gave weapons, four revolvers, to the women inmates, who promised that when the situation changed they would help them in return for the help they had received.

Anxious hours of waiting. Where was the U.S. army? Troubling questions filled the minds of watchful men and women in the uneasy quiet of the camp. Had the SS really gone? Would they be back?

At about 11pm that night a reliable scout reported that the last squads of soldiers had indeed gone. The group leadership took over, giving orders that all receptacles capable of holding water should be filled, in case explosives had been put in place by the departing SS. Prisoners were instructed to maintain calm, self-disciplined behaviour whatever happened. A meeting of fifteen men in Block 24 took place. O'Leary was appointed as chairman. Representatives of twelve nations made decisions on what was best to do, how save the lives of the 32,000 or more still in the main camp, with barely enough food, even if carefully distributed, for twenty-four hours, and no medicines for the thousands who were ill.

Day came. The need to run the camp in an orderly way until Allied forces arrived was explained in each of the barracks. Details of all that must be done were worked out. At around 4.30pm, as well as the deep cannon sounds, they heard, at last, the rattle of machine gun fire. Some shots actually entered the camp. Then the sight they had waited for – at around 5.15 an American combat group, led by a jeep driven by that German Jew who had escaped from the camp, were ecstatically greeted as they drove up. O'Leary and Haulot ran to the gate to greet the American major.

American troops undertook to guard the outside of the camp from any German attack, while O'Leary and Haulot, acknowledged leaders of the camp resistance group, were invested with complete authority to organise the intermediate internal arrangements for the camp. And so, the very last of its roll-calls had already been carried out that morning, when 32,335 including 385 women or children were counted, not as prisoners but as survivors.

Allach camp was liberated at about the same time. Shortly before this happened, a friendly SS man gave two machine guns, and ammunition, to Jews he knew there, telling them that if need be he would fight alongside them. Evacuations were still taking place, chaotic conditions prevailed. The SS had moved out on the night of the 27th, and then an international committee set itself up to maintain order and man the watchtowers until the Americans should arrive. All in all, around 33,000 liberated survivors left Dachau camp, a name and a place synonymous with terror.

CHELMNO, BELZEC, SOBIBOR, TREBLINKA

The death camps – systematic and ruthless; their sole intention the 'final solution', the killing of all Jews.

A line of wire surrounded each camp, covered with branches that concealed the horror within. The arriving thousands were told, this was a transit camp from whence they would be sent to work in the East. Naked and shorn, hurried along the 'tube' leading to the gassing rooms, pushed through airtight doors that cannot be opened from inside – men, then women, the children afterwards, urged into what they think is a shower room, shower-heads in the ceiling disguising the pipes through which deadly gas enters … the heavy doors clang shut.

Chelmno was begun towards the end of 1941, one of the earliest specifically designed to kill; with Jews forced to undertake the procedures of murder. Not infrequently, as the deputy commandant testified at his trial, they refused to do it.

The camp's ending showed that here, too, as in the satirical song a prisoner invented, the zebras, (i.e. those who wore the striped camp uniforms) though they might be lamed, were not tamed. As the liberating Russian troops drew near, the SS ordered the liquidation of the 'labour detail'. During the night of January 14th to 15th 1945, prisoners were taken out five at a time and shot. The cook managed to flee. More executions. That left the upper cell of twenty craftsmen. A police officer went to this upper cell. Four of the prisoners rushed him, pulled him into the cell, snatched his pistol and shot him with it; they set the building alight, and so died.

$$* \quad * \quad *$$

Belzec death camp, built according to the same plan. After careful consideration its commandant decided against using cyanide gas; though efficient, it had to be manufactured in privately owned factories and the vast quantities required for killing hundreds on hundreds of thousands of people might cause unpleasant rumours about what it would be used for.

Carbon monoxide could be obtained on site from the exhausts of large motor vehicles. After testing – on a group of prisoners – this became the method of choice for the extermination camps. But prisoners too weak to walk to the death chambers after their horrific train journey were shot by the guards; deep pits had already been dug to accommodate the piles of human bodies.

With no survivors of the work details at Belzec, only isolated examples of defiance are now known. A group of Polish Jews refused to leave the transport wagons. A woman tried to use a razor blade on a guard. When the camp was obsolescent, and closed down, prisoners transferred to replacement camps saw the same kind of extermination installations. They tried to protest. All were shot, their names not known.

Individuals did escape from work details. One reached freedom in the spring of 1942, to warn his fellow-Jews about what happened in Belzec. Nobody would believe his story.

Sobibor camp opened in March 1942, regarded as an improved version of Belzec.

(Treblinka, its plan identical to that of Sobibor, followed on 23rd July 1942.)

Occasionally someone somehow escaped from Sobibor, determined to warn others. A young Jew went from ghetto to ghetto in Warsaw, telling of the extermination machinery. Still nobody could believe that such things happened, neither then nor when Jews in Berlin heard the facts on BBC radio broadcasts in November 1942.

To anyone in a normal situation, such extremes of abnormality, such hopeless weights of terror, despair and misery would exclude the very idea of resistance. Most of those who went to their deaths from train to gas chamber to crematorium did not get the chance to give their account of how they conducted themselves. What is certain, is that more happened than is known. Some reports indicate that not all were unsuspecting of the fate intended for them. On April 30th 1943, a group of prisoners sent from Wlodawa arriving at the railway's unloading platform at Sobibor attacked the SS and the Ukrainian guards, wounding some of them before being killed. Another group from Minsk, on their arrival in September, pelted the guards with whatever came to hand – stones, bottles, pots, flew through the air. There was a Jew, Shaul Fleischhacker, who came from Kalisz. He is named for his refusal, in that same extermination camp, to beat a fellow inmate. He preferred to take a beating himself.

Prisoners compelled to work there considered how they might make a break for it. According to Simcha Bialowicz, two plans were discussed. In one, prisoners working in the camp kitchen would put poison into the guards' food; in the other plan the barracks would be set on fire, while the inmates skeddadled in the general confusion. The Jewish chief kapo, Moshe, got together with two other kapos, and an uprising was planned, unfortunately betrayed by a fellow Jew, who apparently wanted Moshe's position. If so, he was disappointed, for although he was rewarded with it by the administration after the three uprisers were shot, he did not keep it for long. He was lynched by the other prisoners. The plotting went on.

Leon Feldhendler was such a plotter. A Polish Jew, he drew his own conclusion after Jewish slave labourers brought to the camp in 1943 were killed, as no-longer-needed. Feldhendler had a group around him. Their idea was that with the help of some well-disposed Ukrainian guards from the Soviet Union, they would arrange with partisan groups in the area for collaboration in liberating the camp. Unfortunately the central administration stopped prisoners from working in the kitchens, where a helpful Ukrainian was in charge. But some prisoners, including the Ukrainian Koszewadski, got away, to join up with the partisans. Two more tunnelled their way out, in 1942. Others tried, digging away for many weeks in the summer of 1943, but after that first tunnel the SS took precautions, laying a minefield just outside the wire. The tunnellers broke through, a mine exploded, the SS immediately alerted - one hundred and fifty men were discovered in the tunnel and shot. A group of Dutch Jews planned a mass escape; betrayed by an informer, seventy-one Dutch prisoners died.

The forest detail, where Dutch and Polish Jews worked together, had its escape scenario. Shlomo Podchlebnik and Jozef Kopf, supposed to be fetching water, took the opportunity to beat their guard to death, take his gun and make a run for it. Dutch Jews on that work detail let the SS take them back to the camp, but twenty Polish Jews, well knowing they would be killed anyway, attacked their guards. Eight got away. Local people helped ten escapees, who were not recaptured; the Dutchmen who returned were shot.

Among many escape attempts – made regardless of the terrible consequences for those recaptured – one, given better luck with the weather, might well have succeeded. It was another try at getting out via a tunnel. The group emerged safely outside the wire. That night brought the first snowfall of the year. In the morning the SS tracked footprints in the snow. Caught, the fleeing men fought their pursuers – it is not known for certain if any got away.

A whole transport of Jews, brought from Grodno, refused the order to undress. They called to each other, don't obey, don't go into those rooms camouflaged as showers. They fought, too, rushing the SS with knives and bottles; three injured SS men had to go to hospital for treatment. All 2,000 men and women from that transport were shot. So was Meir Berliner, a young man who'd reached the end of his tether, and a hundred men from his work detail, all shot when the young man stabbed an SS squad leader, who died from his wounds.

The Red Army Jews who arrived in September 1943 from Minsk included officers with partisan experience. Aleksander Pecherskii (there is some doubt about the correct spelling of his name) was a leading figure. An SS guard had offered him cigarettes, and bread, for the way he'd done his work. Pecherskii had proudly refused these rewards. When someone suggested to him that he could escape, he replied that this would lead to reprisals, the better way would be to work out how large numbers of prisoners could escape. Impressed, the resistance group offered Pecherskii the leadership. Thus, a viable team formed, with Feldhendler and Pecherskii on its executive committee.

Rumours came through secret channels that the camp was likely to be closed down. A Ukrainian SS man told a Russian Jew he'd known – they'd served in the army together – of an uprising at Treblinka, and that Sobibor was soon to be liquidated. On the eve of Yom Kippur, the inmates requested and obtained permission from the commandant for prayers to be said in the barracks of Camp 1. The women prayed, loudly, drowning out the voices of Feldhendler's group as they briefed their six hundred fellow-prisoners on a detailed but desperate plan of revolt. Pecherskii informed the Jewish kapos, including them in the planning of the various tasks. On 12th October he held a final leaders' discussion in the carpenter's shop, where the underground committee added the last details to the plans for the uprising and subsequent escape.

The date for the revolt was set as October 14th, when the commandant and his top SS sergeant would be on leave. Only the small planning group knew the exact details of the when and how the outbreak would start.

The blacksmiths had made a dozen small axes. They had knives. Such as they were, these weapons were distributed during the night of the 13th, together with warm clothing. But guns had to be stolen. This task had been entrusted to the children, for they were allowed greater freedom of movement than adults. Youngsters who cleaned the floors and polished the SS men's boots, stole from them whatever they could find in the way of pistols, rifles and hand grenades. They appropriated a sub-machine gun too.

A youth of sixteen, Stanislaw Zmajzner, a plumber, had access to the Ukrainian guards' barracks. There his work installing iron stoves gave him the opportunity to put three rifles into stovepipes, cover these with blankets and deliver them according to his instructions at 3.50pm. (Precise timing was vital, for the SS procedures, like the trains in Germany, ran to time.) Two of the rifles were given to Russian prisoners, Stanislaw kept the other for himself.

Craftsmen-prisoners who made items for the SS guards gave SS men timed appointments to fetch these things from the workshops, or to go one at a time for fittings in the tailor's shop. At the first of these appointments the deputy camp commandant put his gun down while he tried on a garment. It was the last action he ever took. After he was killed, six more SS in the tailor's and shoemaker's shop followed. They had been allocated appointments at fifteen minute intervals after 4.00pm. Each one was punctual, each one was disposed of in his turn. So were four more, from 3.30 onwards, in the store room of Section 2, decoyed there on the pretext of being given a dead prisoner's leather coat. One more was killed in the garage. Other SS men were told that a fellow officer was looking for him, over there, whereas in fact it was the prisoners, and death, that awaited them.

Then a hair-raising moment. One SS man lived long enough after he was stabbed to scream. A prisoner quickly picked up a bell, wildly ringing it to drown out the disastrous sound of those screams. Two Ukrainians rode by on bikes. They too were killed. A German Jew, Schwarz, an electrician, disconnected the lights and the telephone. A little boy ran between Camp 1 and Camp 2 to keep the count of the number of guards killed.

A snag occurred: a SS man unexpectedly drove back to the camp. He wanted his truck unloaded. Unluckily, he saw the newly-dead body of an SS man. Drawing his gun, he fired it at the prisoners. Though he was soon silenced, the sound of the shots had been alarming, disrupting the plan's timing. Another hitch, the camp administrator failed to keep his appointment with death. Rather than go on waiting, the kapo Byetzki was instructed to give the agreed signal for the mass revolt to start.

At the blast of his whistle the prisoners gathered, seventy men, (mostly Russians) in the vanguard. It was no longer possible to fool the guards with the pretence that all was as usual. Pecherskii called out, 'Comrades, forward!' – and with a great shout of 'Hurrah!' Jews from Russia, Poland, Holland, France, Czechoslovakia, Germany, all rushed forward, exhausted as they were, half-starved people attempting to storm the arsenal, stopped by heavy machine gun fire from the SS. They had hoped to win over some of the Ukrainian guards. That part of their plan failed, they must turn about, must make a run for it, run for the fences and the gate. There, a guard with a machine gun, and guards on the towers – though initially stunned by the prisoners' daring – shot and shot again. Determined not to give in, some tore down sections of the barbed wire fence and fled across the minefield outside it. Many were killed, either tangled in the wire or blown up by mines. Others who followed the first ranks climbed over the bodies of their dead comrades to cross the wire.

The committee had made the assumption that the area near to the SS lodgings would not be mined, and those who had been assigned the task of cutting the wire there and getting through, succeeded in making openings – many got clear out of the camp, but at risk from bullets until they got to the sheltering forest. Those prisoners who'd remained in the camp? All shot. The Lublin head of the police department who made out his report gave the time as 5.30. He named it as being an uprising of the Jews in the SS camp Sobibor, states they overpowered the guard, stormed the arms depot, and after a gun fight with the SS, 'fled in an unknown direction', leaving nine SS men killed, one wounded, two foreign guards shot; about 300 Jews escaped.

At the Sobibor trial in September 1965, an SS man giving evidence to the tribunal sitting in judgement stated that about eighty Jews were shot trying to escape, and another thirty or forty had been caught and taken back. On the SS deaths, other evidence showed that as well as the wounded SS men, twenty-one or twenty-three had been killed in the course of the uprising. Of the six hundred Jewish men, women and children at Sobibor, some fifty or sixty survived.

* * *

Ukrainians who'd offered their services as guards staffed the death camp Treblinka. Badly treated by the SS, either their sense of grievance or their desire for gold led to their willingness to trade with the prisoners. The usual trading price for a bottle of schnapps was gold to the value of twenty dollars. Plans of rebellion at Treblinka would include bribery in its strategy, making use of valuables found by prisoners allocated to search the clothes stripped off people before they were gassed.

But in 1942, Jews arriving from Grodno refused to undress and enter the room with the 'showers'. As they broke ranks, they were shot. Despite beatings, others called out to their friends not to obey the orders. Then came an explosion, possibly a hand grenade, severely injuring a Ukrainian guard. The Jews used knives and bottles against the SS in the fight that followed. Three SS men needed hospital treatment. About 2,000 Jews are believed to have taken part in this rebellion. None have lived to tell their own tale, the reprisal shootings took all their lives.

Among many courageous individual acts, four who took a leading part in planning a camp-wide revolt were, a Slovak officer, Zelo Bloch, a Polish kapo Zew Kurland, a Silesian called Lubling and an elderly physician, Julian Chorazycki. Chorazycki was to buy weapons from corrupt Ukrainians guards. Regrettably an SS officer noticed he had a large amount of money in his pocket, and asked him what it was for. The doctor's main concern was not to betray his fellow plotters. He said he was planning to escape, then snatched up a dissecting knife and rushed at the SS man, who managed to deflect the blow, blocking it with a chair. The SS man fell over backwards. Chorazycki swallowed poison, then jumped out of the window. The SS man followed him, whip in hand. After the beating the doctor got, the guards made intensive efforts to revive him, but the combined effects of the beatings and the poison did their work. Dr. Chorazycki died, revealing nothing of the plan.

Others replaced him: Alfred Galewski from Loez, Rudolf Masarek from Prague, (sent to the camp because he refused to leave his Jewish wife) and Stanislaw Lichtblau, a mechanic from Czechoslovakia. Zelo Bloch, the military expert in the group, temporarily lost contact with them; he had been transferred to the other section of the camp. But new strengths came after the Warsaw uprising had been quelled, with men and women survivors arriving hardened from the ghetto struggle. Bringing news that Warsaw's Jews had risen, they could point out it was up to the Treblinka Jews to do likewise.

A way was devised to get access to the SS armoury; first, one of the youngsters, fourteen year old Edek, pushed a piece of metal into the lock, jamming it. The camp locksmith was ordered to repair the lock. As he did so he took an impression, then made a key. About ten groups of between five and ten members were now actively involved in the plan, the two parts of the camp had established links, each group assigned a task. A date for the uprising – June 15th was considered – was difficult to agree on. The younger men, according to Wiernik's account, found it hard to wait.

Stanislaw Kohn, another survivor of the 700 or so who were then at the camp, wrote his account describing the various stages of the plan: first to catch and eliminate the worst of the slave-drivers, then disarm the guards, cut the telephone wires, burn and destroy all the equipment used to murder the prisoners, liberate the penal camp prisoners (Polish men held some 2 kilometres away), join forces with them and head for the forest to form a strong group of partisans.

At last the date was agreed: August 2nd 1943, the time at 5pm. Wiernik let the upper camp know. All who were in the know tried hard to keep to routine in the early part of that day. The young lads could get into the SS barracks – they searched the rooms there, stealing guns and grenades, taking these weapons to the garage area. The distribution of guns was due to begin at 2pm. Infiltrating the SS arsenal came next, when the SS business manager of the camp unexpectedly appeared. The prisoner-agronomist Sudowicz boldly stepped up to him and asked him to kindly inspect some plants – at a sufficient distance for the prisoners' purposes to go ahead.

Malkus and Salzberg had the task of distracting the attention of the arsenal guards, carrying carpets past them, allegedly for cleaning. And the guards turned away for a brief moment. That key, so carefully hoarded, must now instantly work, if all were not to be lost. At the first try it turned in the lock. Jasek, a fourteen year old Hungarian lad, quickly slid in. Tiptoeing to the window on the other side, he cut out a segment with a glass cutter, and through the hole he handed out guns and ammunition. The guns must be hidden in the garage before more SS men turned up. A rubbish collection lorry duly arrived; rubbish, with the guns underneath, was loaded as planned and driven to the garage. Fearing the secret of the rebellion would be out before the set starting time of 5pm, at 4pm instructions from the leadership were sent to all the groups, go immediately to the garage for the issue of weapons. There the password, 'death', would be spoken, with the counterword of 'life' as the reply. Soon the shouts of the password and its response rang out loud and clear.

In the meantime the man who worked as a disinfector of the camp buildings, watched by an SS man who thought he was pouring the usual disinfectant on the barracks, splashed petrol over the wooden huts, ready for the moment, the agreed signal. In the upper camp, co-ordinated action went smoothly. A prisoner held up a gold coin to the Ukrainian guarding the watchtower. Since it was not uncommon for the prisoners to exchange gold for a bottle of schnapps, or even to buy arms, the Ukrainian came down, only to find that the deal was not quite as usual. Instead of the expected lucrative financial deal, he was dealt a blow that knocked him down, and the prisoner grabbed his revolver.

Among the various accounts of what happened next, there is a statement made later to a German court by SS man Suchomel, who came running out of his office in his shirt sleeves, in great astonishment at the sound of exploding hand grenades. He testified that he had looked out of the window and seen Molotov cocktails setting fire to the barracks, a dead informer lying on the ground, prisoners on the ramparts between the two parts of the camp firing shots, the fence being torn down and wooden boards used to get past the tank trap. He saw two guards disarmed, and he heard the shoot-out continue for about a quarter of an hour.

From the upper camp Zelo Bloch broke through by rushing two SS men. Wielding an axe. He took command then of the military action. Leaders of the conspiracy who fought the SS, though dying in the unequal struggle, gave as many of their comrades as possible time to escape. 200 prisoners had been armed, the petrol-soaked barracks were ablaze, fires were everywhere. Whether or not the complete success of the plan was thwarted, as some have said, by the need to bring forward the starting time, the way to freedom had been opened, the fences torn down. Between 150 and 500 got beyond the fence, or reached the forests. They were most fiercely pursued. An unknown number later died fighting as partisans, while, most tragic of all, some were killed by anti-Semitic Poles. (Poland's complicated history is involved in such events. Going back to the 14th century, the then king, Kazimierz the Great invited Jews to settle in Poland to improve its economic and cultural life. By 1939 Jews formed about 10% of the population, living mainly in urban areas, with Yiddish as their first language and keeping up their religious rituals and ways of dressing. When Poland's regime experienced severe problems with the economy, it was easy to scapegoat such a recognisable minority. Anti-Semitic policies were further exacerbated by Nazi propaganda, which fitted with the Nazi-style government. So it is all the more to the credit of Poles who nonetheless helped and sheltered Jews despite the peril to themselves; not a few hidden Jewish children owe their lives to such Polish rescuers.)

The prosecutors who prepared the post-war Treblinka trial in Dusseldorf reported that fifty men and two women who escaped did live to see the end of the Nazi regime. Some who made good their escape set about letting the world know about Treblinka. In 1944, with Warsaw still occupied, a secret publishing enterprise produced and distributed 2,000 copies of Yankel Wiernik's experiences, written while he was hidden by Polish friends. Copies of Wiernik's report were sent to London and the USA. A Georg Rajgrodzki got to Warsaw, sheltered by a German woman who had a Czech husband. Another German, Fritz Müllhoff, looked after two of the Treblinka escapees as well as helping other underground fugitives evade the Gestapo's attentions.

Richard Glazar has written a report of those extraordinary events at Treblinka on that August day in 1943; with the significant comment that the flames to be seen then, rising higher than those usually seen at the crematorium, were also different in colour, of a different origin, and were to be interpreted differently than those of any previous night. The camp's extermination machinery was, though seriously damaged, not entirely destroyed. It was put to its evil use for a few last transports of Bialystok Jewry. At the end of November 1943 the telltale installations were completely demolished, the prisoners killed.

AUSCHWITZ – BIRKENAU

Auschwitz–Birkenau's buildings and installations sprawled over twenty-five square miles. Set up in 1940, in 1943 the administration was split into Auschwitz 1, Auschwitz 2, (that was Birkenau) and Auschwitz 3 (that was Monowitz). Subsidiary camps, either at or conveniently near arms factories, quarries or chemical works, came under that vast umbrella. Monowitz served I.G. Farben industries, owners of the Buna Rubber Works; there Primo Levi's skills as a chemist were exploited while he was a half-starved prisoner, number 174517.

The Polish resistance movement had an active base near Auschwitz. Polish prisoners smuggled out information to these anti-Nazis in the first year of the camp; escapees had hopes of joining a partisan group. Then thirty assorted characters, including some outstandingly good or bad people, were transferred from Dachau to Auschwitz, to run it for the SS. A Bruno Brodniewicz, number 1, was exempt from the otherwise universal requirement to wear a coloured triangle. For services rendered to the regime? Hermann Langbein comments on what he calls the heinous deeds of this number 1; adding that, unlabelled, his criminal past was evident only from his demeanour. On the other hand, number 2, Otto Küsel, though wearing a green triangle, and with a 'soft' job in the labour records office, took no advantage of the power his position gave him. Eventually he took positive action, joining in an escape, and what an escape, one like the plot of a Hollywood film: 'Colditz, eat your heart out.'

On the numbers between 2 and 14, I learned nothing of their individual attitudes and quirks. Number 14, who was German, was recalled by Primo Levi. Otto, proud of being a camp veteran, heavy handed, carrying out his duties roughly, but not counted as one of the worst. Levi fashioned a memorable story-account of an encounter between Otto and a highly religious Jew.

In this story a prisoner called Ezra realised that the next day, for those who lived to see it, would be Yom Kippur – the Jewish day of atonement for one's sins, and forgiveness for the sins of others. A day of fasting. Ezra, who'd been a watchmaker in a Lithuanian village before arriving at Auschwitz, felt an urgent need to keep his soul together as well as his body. After the weariness of the day's work came the line-up for the ration of soup. Ezra amazed Otto, and no doubt all within earshot, by speaking up instead of holding out his mess tin for the ladle of soup.

His voice low and respectful, his request unprecedented, he explained that as that evening began the day of atonement, Ezra was by his religion forbidden to eat anything; he was asking for his ration of soup to be saved so he could have it on the following evening. This was the first time in Otto's seven years of camp experience that anyone had refused food. Ezra was told to step aside, wait until the food was served out. And then he was interrogated by Otto on these strange requirements of laws, so imperative that Ezra took the risk of horrendous punishment by asking for them to override the SS rules. They discussed the issue; Ezra explained his stance, Otto agreed to save the filled mess tin until Ezra came for it the following evening. Whatever brief or longer-lasting ray of light shone for those prisoners who came to tell each other that story when, for instance, they were carrying bags of cement from one warehouse to another, must be guessed at. Other groups of pious Jews, in spite of being forbidden, did on days of significance chant as religion required, gathering together on Friday evenings, where in darkness they softly sang the Sabbath songs or debated whether they should or should not eat or work on the day of atonement. Many other Jews, including Kitty Felix and Daniella Raphael, and even, after a long time, the ultra-religious Rena Kornheim, ceased to have a religious faith, abandoning the idea of a God who, had he existed, would have appeared to have abandoned them; they survived, not on faith but on friendship's help, freely given, when such acts as propping the weakest up to get through the roll-call, protect one nearly dead from a whipping, use secret devices and arrangements, made it possible to maintain the inner resistance necessary for survival.

The first political prisoners who arrived, Polish army officers, maintained strict notions of precedent based on rank. One, Witold Pilecki, had got himself arrested during a raid in Warsaw in September 1940, his aim and intention to set up a secret military organisation in the camp. His own name would have been too dangerous, he'd acquired papers in the name of Tomas Serafinski. Once inside he set himself to form The Union of the Military Organisation, tight-knit groups of five, sworn to loyalty, who helped each other with extra food and clothing (the first necessity) and created battle-ready groups. The Polish Government-in-Exile received a first report from this group on March 18th 1941. A few members, when conditions allowed, later organised escapes. Army officers if detected were shot – it was a risky business for Polish officer-groups to insist on addressing each other by their army rank, ignoring the likelihood of being overheard; a host of spies and informers served the so-called 'political department'. Very daring was Pilecki's 1941 plan for a military uprising. Attempting to convince partisans that his plan was feasible, (and also because his own situation had become perilous) Pilecki escaped from the bakery, situated outside the camp boundary, making contact with the Polish underground.

Then after June 1941 the Spanish group's activities came to the fore. These were prisoners, many of them communists, who had fought in the Spanish civil war, then, fleeing to France, had been interned and finally sent on to German camps. Their organisation was formed on the day Germany attacked the Soviet Union. Its aims included those spelled out by the Poles, but included the wider tasks of appointing trusted people to positions where they could gather information and observe the SS, seek contacts with prisoners of other nationalities, strengthen confidence in the democratic nations' ability to achieve the victory over Fascism, and play their part in this victory by taking any opportunity to sabotage or go-slow on German war work.

Russian prisoners who arrived, if alive, if not immediately shot or gassed, were assigned to hard labour. Fed on substitute bread, POW bread baked from a special recipe, 50% rye husks, 20% chopped sugar beets, 20% ground cellulose, 10% ground straw or leaves, and in the evening, half a litre of soup, doled out after their twelve-hour shifts in the armament factories, few survived for any length of time. (In the autobiography of Höss, the then commandant, a man brutal even by SS standards, he recalls how Russian prisoners building Birkenau, died like flies from exhaustion and shockingly unhealthy conditions.) In desperation, they planned a mass breakout, probably in March 1942. One hundred and twenty got out, but one hundred and three are thought to have died. And in her memoir, Rena Kornreich records how when she arrived at Auschwitz, (numbered 1716, still thinking it was a work camp from which she would be released) the group she came with had to wear the bullet-holed clothes of just-dead Russian prisoners of war – throughout the night she heard the shooting of many more prisoners.

In the Autumn, witnesses of another escape described the Russians' plan. The body of a prisoner was hidden, so that the roll call numbers did not tally; this looked like an escape attempt to the guards. A search for the missing man began – the Russians volunteering for the job. Dark night, and fog – the volunteers toppled a watch tower and broke out. At least four survived. After this Russians repeatedly tried to get out, one group of eleven succeeding. Exceptionally daring, they boosted their strength by working always as a group.

A different stance was taken by Jehovah's Witnesses, conscientious objectors on religious grounds, who neither fought nor tried to escape. Nor would they do any work useful to the German army or air force, despite severe punishments. Miniature Bibles, smuggled-in with illegally printed copies of 'The Watchtower', Sunday afternoon prayer meetings with brethren standing watch in case SS men came along, helped them maintain their staunch opposition to Fascism, their unity and care for each other. A specially composed song circulated, bringing them comfort. Survivor's accounts confirm that these attitudes prevailed in various camps where Witnesses were held, often isolated from other prisoners.

Gypsies, allocated special numbers and, like 'anti-socials' and criminals, also kept as isolated as possible, were labelled with triangles of black. (The only group denied a country, their survivors were the only group not to receive compensation.) It was known these Gypsies had been troublesome in Buchenwald, where many perished during the first winter of the war. But they maintained their firmness, refusing to beat a Frenchwoman they were ordered to punish with twenty-five blows. Their children taken away from them, they refused to turn out for the daily roll call; the trucks came, to load them all, take everyone to the gas chambers. Other prisoners nearby heard cries that sounded like 'Criminals! Murderers!' Then shots. Next morning, the empty section. Bloodstains. No more. (A tale of experiences in Auschwitz was written by a later Roma detainee there; from an educated family, he had travelled widely before being picked up in Hungary when that country was invaded. Made to work under the infamous Mengele, his language skills kept him alive as an interpreter. He did manage to escape, finding shelter not far from the camp.)

Some of the 'red triangle' German prisoners were using positions they'd gained as vantage points, opportunities for opportunists and for planners, disseminators of an alternative approach, organisers of resistance. Others proved less resistant to corroding influences, regrettably taken over by the Führer principle. An increasing amount of administration work devolved onto prisoners as the camp spread, and continued to spread. The capacity of the gas chambers and crematoria proved insufficient for the size of the set task. On Himmler's orders, four more crematoria were added, their built-in gas chambers an innovation. The process of mass murder was supposed to be a closely guarded secret. To prevent knowledge of it leaking out the 'political department' used more informers at Auschwitz than in any other camp – though the efforts of prisoners would foil them.

The gas used from 1941 – sometimes it was injected – called Zyclon B, is hydrocyanic acid, prussic acid. The Nazis used techniques already tried out with the 'euthanasia' project T4 (named from the address of the Co-ordinating Office at Tiergarten-strasse 4, Berlin). Records show 90,000 lives taken, in Brandenburg, in Bensburg, in Grafeneck, in Hartheim, in Hadamar, in Sonnenstein, in Eichberg. (The project's head officer, SS-Major Christian Wirth, later took charge at Sobibor before being promoted to Auschwitz.)

Gas as the method of choice followed from experience gained when thousands, hundreds of thousands, of German Jews were taken from Germany to Riga, made to undress, jump into pits, lie down close together in neat rows ready be shot; the next lot had to jump in, lie on top of them and… and even then the quantities of the dead weren't enough. And bullets were expensive. Hence the newly designed gas chambers; with crematoria attached, no time would be wasted transferring bodies from one place to another.

The procedure of using carbon monoxide pumped into shower cubicles through nozzles had worked well on the 'mental patients' and 'unfit' of the earlier experiments, but Eichman rejected it for Auschwitz on the grounds that its mass use would require too many new buildings; and getting such enormous quantities of the gas was considered to be a logistical problem. His new Zyclon method involved teams of trained prisoners with the official name 'the disinfectors', supplied with working tools, canisters about the size from the floor to a person's knees, a hammer, quite a heavy hammer, weighing between two and five pounds. A flat roof, designed to be easily stood on, of what was called the bathhouse, so when the doomed prisoners, three hundred or so at a time, were told to strip off for a shower, crammed in, the doors fastened shut on them, onto the roof climbed the 'special unit's' disinfectors.

It was then that the prisoner-unit must put the point of the opener on the lid of the canister raise the hammer bring it down to pierce the drum. Then, the canister open, the special mechanism for lowering the canister into each of the gassing areas, two ducts, four iron pipes running from floor to roof, the canister filled with gas crystals to be lowered by the attached wire. Down into the room. Close off the roof space. Safe then for the disinfectors to take off the SS issue gas masks. Screams from below, banging on the walls, would be heard. For five minutes. Then the doors would be opened, the bodies pulled out. Next, lot, next, next. In the Autumn of 1942 Jews were transferred from camps using less efficient facilities for killing the 100,000 Jewish men, 50,000 Jewish women listed. All Gypsies too, were now declared 'unfit to live'.

The army's losses and reversals on the Eastern front led to administrative and policy changes; now camps operated according to the directions of the SS Main Economic and Administrative Office, which decreed that all manpower must be utilised for military purposes. This resulted in sub-camps sited near arms factories – they grew fast as weeds. The first women sent to Auschwitz, in March 1942, laboured at building Birkenau before being transferred there. As one of the longest-surviving of these, Rena Kornreich, would later testify, conditions in Birkenau were much worse than at Auschwitz.

Desperate people from Birkenau's penal colony made mass attempts at freedom. On June 20th 1942 about fifty Polish men broke out. Nine managed to get away, thirteen were shot, the rest captured and killed. So were three hundred innocent bystanders as reprisals followed, always a problematic element in the decision as to whether an escape attempt should be made or not. A group of fourteen Jews deported from France tried. All that is known now of this, is that all were shot – I record this ghost of their story here, to help keep its faint memory alive. Another group of young Jews, some of them communists, were transferred from Buchenwald in 1942 – about 600 assigned to leave that October. When all personal items were taken from them, they concluded, with good reason, that they were on route for the crematorium. At the roll call before they left, some brave souls broke through the surrounding cordon of block leaders. Knocking them to the ground, they ran through the camp shouting that they would not let themselves be slaughtered, they wanted to die fighting. Accounts of this revolt differ about numbers and details, but all agree that the camp management, instead of taking the expected reprisals, calmed the prisoners down. A report from Auschwitz put the number of those from the 600 arriving there at 454; of whom forty-one lived to be liberated.

In another subsidiary camp, Jaworzno, the nearness of a forest (only some fifty metres from the camp's perimeter) suggested the suitability of tunnelling a way out. Using the plan of an experienced mason, digging at night, with the collusion of a senior block inmate, a Czech called Karel Bulaty, they dumped dredged-up sand underneath the block, levelling it underneath the flooring. Civilian clothes, money, all arranged. It had the makings of a successful breakout – but someone told the SS. Mass punishments, tortures and transfers to Buchenwald, hangings of twenty six Poles and Czechs followed. The informer? He was lynched by prisoners after they, and he also, were transferred to Buchenwald.

Then in 1942 an epidemic of typhus. Seventeen prisoners, politicals from Dachau, where they had worked together in the infirmary, were requisitioned to help stop the spread of typhus (after all, it might spread to the guards). Appointed to positions in Auschwitz's infirmary, they could act as a group. A group could achieve things not possible for an individual.

One of the transferred prisoners, Hermann Langbein, had been told, by a man held in Dachau, an Austrian called Josef Lauscher, of a name, a reliable person he should seek out when he was transferred, he must find Ernst Burger.

Ernst Burger and Langbein were to build an organisation in Auschwitz that would overcome ingrained notions of status and nationality that had previously played into the hands of the SS State. Their resistance group and its offshoots would succeed in saving many lives.

As clerk in the infirmary, Langbein first studied how he might influence the German doctor in charge, Dr. Eduard Wirths. Wirth's behaviour was ambiguous. He took part in mass murders, he conducted medical experiments. But Langbein detected in him an inner opposition. a medical conscience. Langbein told him his subordinates were killing weak patients in the hospital. Wirths put a stop to it.

Up to that time only non-medically trained prisoners were assigned to hospital work. Langbein persuaded Wirths to ask for imprisoned doctors. At first these were non-Jews. Langbein then dared to make the suggestion that Jewish physicians from newly-arriving transport trains could be useful – Wirths immediately saw these must be segregated so they would not treat any Aryan prisoners – and with this proviso, Jewish doctors, as they lined up for the initial selection, were pulled out of the line, to be assigned to hospital duties. After some eighteen months Langbein could reveal to Wirths that a secret resistance group was at work in the camp and that he, Langbein, spoke for and acted on decisions reached by this group.

Despite the selections, the camp swelled, crowded with 100,000 Jewish men, 50,000 Jewish women. Women prisoners sent from Ravensbrück were also forced to help build the women's camp. One woman, Vera Alexander, soon had to face up to the dilemma of how best to help her fellow inmates. Another Slovak Jew, Katja Singer, a roll-call clerk, asked Vera to take on the job of block clerk. Vera at first refused, dreading any involvement in keeping the system running. Katja urged on her that it was better, when this could be done, to have influential positions filled by good people. Vera found she was indeed able to help, ensuring each person in her block got the few items allocated to prisoners; she managed, too, to hide sick women so they escaped a death-sentence selection, or hide someone sentenced to death.

Yet another unexpected episode disrupted the power-structure, on December 29th, 1942. Otto Küsel, the German who bore the number 2, in a privileged position due to his nationality, his long-standing residency, his post as head of Work Assignments, astonishingly skipped, along with three Polish members of his work gang.

The three Poles stole an SS uniform. Küsel requisitioned a farm wagon, which he drove into the camp. Hidden in chests, the escapees were loaded aboard. Küsel drove the wagon out of the camp, without any search by the guards. One of the escapers then put on the SS uniform and sat beside Küsel. At the next checkpoint, the uniformed one showed the pass they had organised, which permitted him to escort one prisoner past the gate. The timing was good, with many of the SS on leave. Polish help had been arranged, they reached Warsaw safely. It was only many months later that Küsel was arrested there by the Gestapo, returned, and, after the obligatory torture, transferred to Flössenberg camp.

Küsel's reasoning, as he later explained in his own account, was that either he must flee with the Polish officers who had told him their intention or he must denounce them, to escape punishment for not doing so. He didn't wish to denounce anyone, so he chose to join the escape.

When in 1942 Jewish women from various countries were grouped in Birkenau, some of these recent arrivals tried escaping. Thirteen were shot just outside the camp. Many not in any organisation took the only action they could conceive of, dodging the guards to seize the wire of the electric fence, choosing their own death. In the satellite camp Gleiwitz 4, a group of about ten women who had secretly organised in the ghetto at Lodz continued to work as a group. Besides helping each other, they helped others whenever they could. Some of the most active prisoners were Jews who also wore the 'political' triangle. Even as Jews, they were at great risk of harsh treatment; despite their double risk, Jewish veterans of the Spanish War, of various nationalities, played a full part in the camp resistance movement. At the satellite camp Monowitz, communist Jews, German and Austrian, who had known what it was to endure Buchenwald, formed a group which became active in October 1942. Those Jewish comrades must have been keen communists, for they regarded their resistance organisation as a communist party branch. When a nineteen year old lad called Fritz Kleinmann, who had been transferred to Monowitz with them, revealed not a single name under torture, the group did him the singular honour of offering him membership of the party as a reward for his loyalty.

The desire to get accurate information out of the camp constituted a strong motive for planning escapes, despite the dreaded SS reprisals. When in 1942 a somewhat less vicious commandant was appointed – partly as a result of information smuggled out and broadcast on BBC radio, partly as the war situation made the Nazis uneasy – the Polish resistance revised its previous ban on escapes, instructing Kazimierz Halon to try it, for the purpose of publicising full details of conditions in the camp. On February 20th 1943 he succeeded. Hidden in a Cracow flat, he was told not to leave it until he had completed as detailed a report as he could possibly compile, including a map of the main camp, the satellite camps of Birkenau, Radjsko, and Budy. All this to be passed on to the Allies.

News also arrived at Cracow that a large number of deportees from Hungary had fled as the transport trains were unloaded on May 25th and 28th, only to be shot while hiding in a copse. That information was provided by the newly formed Combat Group Auschwitz, a group which moved on from a Polish Nationalist standpoint, playing a much greater part in resistance after achieving an international viewpoint. Josef Cyrankiewicz, a leader of the Socialist Party in Cracow, is credited with playing an outstanding part in overcoming national selfishness, advocating solidarity and international co-operation. After a group of Polish Socialists, working independently of the military groupings, had managed to send information out through civilian workers, the 'political department' found out and shot the group's leader, Stanislaw Dubois. But Cyrankiewicz, because of his Cracow connections, was able to strengthen the group's contact with opposition still functioning outside. Cyrankiewicz it was who made contact with Austrians like Langbein, who in turn suggested they could form an international group, merging the Polish group with the Austrian, which already included French, Czech and Jewish comrades, then adding the Russians and Germans. That day, 1st May, 1943, a rare holiday – the SS guards off-duty, prisoners talking to each other within the camp. Tentative arrangements made, later formalised, as the respected Viennese Ernst Burger agreed with the decision, go ahead with collaboration between groups, fully merge in one united organisation. Emphatically, they did not wish to work as national groups any more, but to organise teams made up of people of mixed nationality and assorted political opinions.

Burger was a man, in his free life an official of a communist youth association, who won liking and respect from all for his calm helpfulness. Though classed, like all Austrians, as German, and with a position as block clerk, he did not take advantage for himself of a potentially corrupting power position. (Later on, he and Langbein both took the precaution of talking things over together or with someone they could rely on, checking on their actions to ensure they were not being unwittingly sucked into serving the turn of the SS.) Burger had been transported to Auschwitz in the December of 1941; he excelled in creating a network of contacts. He'd met Janez Ranziger on the way, and they'd kept in touch, Ranziger appreciative of the radio news passed on to him. They became aware of a Russian group led by Major Alexander Lebedev. A French-speaking prisoner made the link, the contact both groups sought. By retaining a Polish leader, someone known to the Polish Resistance, the group was in a sound position to make contact with civilian Polish workers employed at the camp. Letters passed to and fro, incoming ones quickly destroyed. Prudence suggests the out-going letters would also be considered too incriminating to keep. On Langbein's evidence, the Cracow group, daring or rash or just clever at it, preserved three hundred and fifty letters from this two-way exchange; information on what help escapees would most need when they got out, and information for the Polish organisation to send on to London, which did get through. From Cracow it reached London. Höss was sacked from his commandant's job, possibly as a result of someone's conviction that if facts broadcast on Allied radios were believed, someone so notorious could be a liability to his bosses in the event of post-war trials.

SS reprisals became less horrific, to help a prisoner escape less agonising, though an escape of three Poles brought equivocal results. With reason to fear their connection with the contact network would be discovered by the political department, the three had drugged a guard they were 'on terms' with. They got clear away, but the shootings and hangings that followed gave their story a sad and sorry ending.

Hitler's birthday in 1943 was marked by the arrival at the women's section of Birkenau of many Jews rounded up in Berlin. Among this contingent were Danielle Raphael and her mother. After ups and downs in the early weeks there, Danielle, saved time and time again from a death situation by her mother's efforts and the kindness of well-disposed friends, found herself moved to a relatively safe job in the laundry, washing clothes for the SS. The women in that work detail helped with her share of the washing until she regained her strength, and could not only do her own share but in her turn help out weaker women. Her friends there even had a few possessions; each had a comb, a toothbrush, a handkerchief. On the eve of her 21st birthday she had saved food items from the first Red Cross parcel that came for her, intending to treat her friends to a special party delicacy, by sharing among them the tin of Red Cross sardines she'd hidden away. Alas, all her treasures were confiscated in an SS search. She relates how, by the morning, her friends had organised replacements. One woman donated her own scarcely used toothbrush, one found her a handkerchief. And amongst the goodies, a tin of sardines. When this was opened and shared out, it went further than any tin of sardines they'd ever known. Though these women, and others in the clothes-sorting work detail known as 'Kanada', were not organised into a resistance group their efforts as they helped each other to survive, their friendship, mark them as true resisters of the State power holding them in its grip.

The newly appointed commandant stopped the gas-chamber selections of the infirm, so when in January 1944 Langbein heard that another such selection was imminent, on behalf of the Combat Group he urged Dr. Wirths to tell the commandant what was going on. As it turned out, the commandant knew. Orders had come directly from Berlin, too many prisoners in the camp were not fully fit for work, so eight hundred had been selected from patients already in the hospital, three hundred more from the camp. The representations made by Doctor Wirths to the commandant, urged on as he was by Hermann Langbein, resulted in reprieve for the three hundred Jews who'd been selected in the camp and already isolated in readiness for the gas chambers – released to the utter amazement of relatives and friends, who had thought them beyond help. Moreover, the commandant had agreed that only the terminally ill should be selected; Wirth's examination of the hospitalised got that number down to three hundred. A marked-out prisoner's life could also be saved by removing his tattooed number, replacing it with that of a prisoner already dead, the saved person then known in the camp by the name of the dead person.

The Polish military organisation, which had been weakened by mass arrests towards the end of 1943, now listened to the opinion of the Polish Social Democrats, that they should co-operate organisationally with the Combat Group. Early in 1944 disagreements on policy, tactics and temperament were put aside, replaced with the overriding idea, co-operation to save lives, oppose the SS state, retain human dignity.

Not only in the main camp, but in satellite camps such as Birkenau, the international group spread its influence. This motley group struggled on, its leading figures determined to cut across boundaries made up of ingrained prejudices, its members an incongruous cross-section of assorted souls thrown together by whatever chances or choices life had confronted them with. The number of escapees rose; regaining freedom was no longer an unthinkable event. By 1943, three hundred and ten had got out, and half of these got away. The escape figures reflect the success of the Combat Group in providing maps, food, medicines, bribery of SS guards, devising secret places where escapers could hide on their way through the checkpoints to the outside of the closely guarded camp. The Polish resistance, some of whom had themselves made successful escapes, maintained their bases near the camp, in a good position to help new escapees. A Polish family might be willing to hide a fugitive. Polish farmers might act to show sympathy. Rena Kornreich gratefully records an incident when a farmer drove his cartful of cabbages across a nearby field, jerking the horse's reins as he passed by, so that the animal's response caused five cabbages to roll off, fresh green juicy leaves collected and distributed by the women who washed the SS underpants.

Herr Himmler would not have been pleased. He was considerably upset by reports of the growing number of escapees.

In October 1943, on the 23rd, all in the camp were to learn that SS men were also mortal. One thousand seven hundred Jews deported from Warsaw to Bergen-Belsen were told they would be moved from there to Switzerland – too many were getting to know what happened at Auschwitz for their true destination to be revealed. After their arrival about two-thirds did enter the gas chambers before they realised where they were. Then rebellion broke out in the undressing room. The prisoners cut the electricity supply wires, they seized the SS weapons, attacked the guards and stabbed one to death. In darkness they shot it out, a second SS officer seriously injured. The commandant arrived, with searchlights. He ordered the doors shut. The prisoners were penned into a corner, brought out individually to be shot – stories and rumours of more revolts, with none left to bear witness, were rife.

The spring of 1944 saw several escapes by Czech and Slovak Jews. Viteszlav Lederer had been an officer in a secret Czech military group, alas not secret enough, for it was betrayed to the Germans. Lederer had survived his arrest, made as long ago as 1939, moved on from one prison to another, repeatedly tortured in attempts to get information out of him, sent to Theresienstadt, then on December 19th 1943 to Auschwitz. Even after his appointment as senior block inmate in the family camp, the interrogation sessions continued.

Here an SS man comes into his story. This man, Victor Pestek, a German from Rumania, assigned to bring Lederer for further questioning whenever the 'political department' required him, found out that sooner or later Lederer, as a Jew accused of political crimes, would be executed.

Pestek's disgust for it all led to a plan cooked up between himself and Lederer. Lederer knew a lot of people in Czechoslovakia, and might help Pestek to drop out of sight there if he, Pestek, helped him, Lederer, to escape. Agreement on the detail was soon reached. Pestek got hold of papers and an SS uniform for Lederer's disguise, and hey presto, the unlikely alliance succeeded. They got to Prague. Lederer desperately tried to warn the Jews in Theresienstadt what would happen to them if they let themselves be transported to Auschwitz. They would not believe him. They thought their town camp was too valuable to the Nazis' propaganda campaign for anything so awful to happen to them. All Lederer could do was to try the Red Cross in Switzerland. Not all escapees could, like Wetzler and Vrba, have the satisfaction of being believed in a world that on the whole prefers not to see or hear or understand.

Messages: the Combat Group specified targets for bombing raids. On June 24th 1943, a letter from them tells of an enormous factory being built next to the blocks in the camps, of machinery already being installed, adding, the writer believes the birds ought to fly to that target in a month's time, and not hold back because prisoners were living there, the firm of Krupps should be destroyed, razed to the ground. Another message asked for the gas chambers and crematoria to be bombed too, and the railway station.

The Combat Group used the growing weakness of the SS, devising ways to send out names and details of the camp murderers. The BBC broadcast warnings that named persons would be held responsible for their actions. A perceptible easing of conditions followed, while one notorious member of the political department hastily changed his name, and got a new paybook. After the trial of officers who attempted to kill Hitler in 1944, the Combat Group issued a statement in reply to the claim by made by the presiding Judge – Roland Freisler – that only criminals were detained in concentration camps. Proudly, the Group informed the free world of their existence, and their unequal struggle for the rights of all political prisoners.

The outflow of information continued. Vera Foltynova, a Czech woman, is credited with getting the plans – hastily copied in the dark, one eye on the door in case the guard came in – showing the extended gas chambers complete with crematoria, her drawings smuggled out from the camp's construction office, sent to Bohemia and to Poland. The death statistics were sent to contacts in Vienna by the camp's Austrian resistors. Determined to find more ways to convince the world outside that their reports of genocide were genuine, in 1944 the Combat Group Auschwitz sent out an urgent request for two rolls of metal film for a specified camera. Why? With so much disbelief, the group took the enormous risks involved in backing up their reports with photographs showing dead bodies, people gassed, people being burned.

How else could the outside world learn, while still the war went on, of what was happening in Auschwitz? At Birkenau, a Polish woman, Krystyna Zywulska, met women held for minor offences, who were about to be discharged. Trusting to one of these, she sewed a description of the extermination process into her garter. The woman agreed to take it to Krystyna's relatives in Warsaw. A covering letter asked for three boiled eggs to be sent in a food parcel, as a sign that the information had been received. And this was done.

An Austrian Jewish doctor managed to bury his collected data on figures of arrivals, gassings and other murders. These were later retrieved. And much detailed information came from people who escaped. Two young Jews were to get out of Birkenau. One was Alfred Wetzler, the other Walter Rosenberg, best known as Rudolf Vbra, the name he assumed after deportation from Slovakia in 1942. Vbra's story contains many elements, there was much to do before his eventual escape with Wetzler. Even before he was put on the train for the concentration camp, his cousin, a girl of thirteen, heard he'd been arrested. What could she do? What she did was to grab the few pence she had, rush to the shop, for whatever her money could buy, then run to the railway station, just in time to give him – a few cherries. Wonderful child. In the camp too, help came, help given before he knew it was so, before he made contact with the network of underground resistors. When he did he took part. And that could have its harrowing tasks, as he was to find out in his dealings with Fredy Hirsch. This was after Jews from Terezin, or Theresienstadt, family camp had been despatched to Auschwitz. Children in the group were looked after by a German Jew, Fredy Hirsch. Well looked after by Fredy, who got them the use of a barracks as a school – he made out he would teach them German – and childish activities there gave the children relief, they loved Fredy. But it fell to Rudolf Vrba to learn, through the camp's secret methods, that an order was made out for these children and their families to be exterminated.

He tells Hirsch. He suggests, those adults who are strong enough should stage a revolt, they have nothing to lose, they might get some of the guards before they were killed. He does not expect the bitter argument that follows, for Hirsch sees such an action by him as participating in the organised death of the children, he cannot bear to think of himself as their betrayer. He asks for an hour to think over Vrba's plan. And when Vrba comes back in one hour for the answer, he finds Hirsch. On the floor. Unable to make the choice, he had swallowed Luminol. There is no revolt, no signal to other parts of the camp to take action. The members of the family camp are all marched to their death – but a survivor of the special unit, Filip Muller, reported that as they calmly marched to the gas chambers, they began to sing.

Mala Zimetbaum, a young Jewish woman, has a story well-remembered by survivors. Mala was a personality – well-liked, cheerful, confident, her knowledge of languages invaluable for her work as a messenger in the camp. She linked up separated families. She organised medicines, she would warn patients to leave the hospital quickly, if she'd found out that another selection for the gas chambers was on the cards. She always tried to send the half-recovered to the lightest sort of work. Whenever a problem came up, Mala would listen, Mala would help. Mala was known as kindness and patience personified. There are many accounts of her escape attempt with a Polish friend, Edward Galinski. Mala had organised a pass, from the office of the women's section. Galinski wore an SS uniform, he pretended he was escorting his girl friend. The two were allowed through the checkpoints. Polish friends helped them, they reached the Slovakian border. Before they could cross to safety a patrol spotted them. Caught by sheer bad luck, they were brought back. Mala, tortured, would not name names. Brought out to be publicly hanged she stood calmly, even smiling, before the assembled prisoners in the main square where the gallows loomed. Somehow, from somewhere, from somebody, she'd obtained a razor blade. Before the guards could stop her, she'd pulled the blade out of her sleeve and slashed her wrists. Witnesses record the furious anger of the SS, how

Mala hit one of them in the face with her bloodstained hand, the accusing words she cast at them, calling them murderers, shouting to them not to touch her, as her blood flowed out. She was loaded onto a hand-cart, her friends ordered to push it along the camp street for everyone to see, on her way straight to the crematorium. One witness, Rena Kornreich, and another, Kitty Felix, who survived, recalled how they all hoped Mala would be dead before she was thrown into the oven. Rena later heard a rumour that an SS guard had ensured this, by shooting her as she lay on the handcart, her arms trailing over the sides. Mala's last defiant words to the SS had been, that they were doomed, their days were numbered – words remembered, though many years passed before Kitty could relate them in her own tale of survival.

Kitty's will to live on, to disobey within herself, triumphed, as she herself says, because she had her mother in the camp to help her over each crisis, and she had her mother to help in her turn. To be helped and to help, not ever to steal from the living though to keep on living by taking from those already dead, became part of her self-articulated set of rules. Rena too, with her young sister to protect, lived her camp existence with the notions of fairness regulating her personal behaviour, she shared scraps of food she'd organised, long after her childhood-inculcated Jewish faith withered on the vine. She no longer fasted on the day of Yom Kippur, she fasted when her share of bread was even more intensely needed by someone appealing to her for help. From her first day in the camp, when a Polish prisoner had called across to her, asking, what did she need, and supplying her with a piece of rope and a nail, this girl of nineteen survived right from the time of the first Jewish transport to Auschwitz, survived the death march out, survived to liberation, holding out and holding on, by giving and receiving help. When she was near to breaking, at the end, her little sister took over her role. Though their parents died, though many of their family died, the Kornreich sisters lived on, married and emigrated to the United States, raising families there.

At Birkenau David Szmulewski, a Polish Jew, a veteran of the Spanish Civil War, held a leading position in the underground movement, liasing between the Combat Group and the special unit. Also André Mandryckxs, a remarkable and outstanding person, described as 'a fine lad'. Roza Roboza, who had a Zionist education. Her story concerns help she gave to the resistance movement by smuggling explosives out of the munitions factory. Roza spoke with young Jewish girls working at the factory, who turned themselves into successful smugglers. We know the 'special unit' made excellent use of the explosive materials: they blew up a crematorium, as part of a planned rebellion.

It was Samuel Lewental who described – in his buried description of his hated life in the special detail – how the idea of rebellion was ever-present. Early in May 1944, extensive preparations were being made to burn Jews from Hungary. Every member of the detail, from the best of them to the worst of them, decided to put a stop to their own participation. Two had emigrated in 1931 from Poland to France, had been active in the French resistance before being arrested by the Gestapo, then sent to Auschwitz in March 1943. These were Dorebus, (using the name Josel Warszawski,) and Jankiel Handelsman, both with good contacts with the resistance movement, and they took the lead in the planned rebellion. Timing was a matter for anxious discussion, as nearby partisan groups doubted they would be able to give shelter to a large number of fugitives, while the Combat Group Auschwitz had reservations about the chances for a successful general struggle at that time. The special detail men wanted to act. The numbers allocated to the detail increased, by May 16th 1945 nine hundred and fifty two listed, from Hungary, from Poland, from Greece, from Russia, a German kapo – these increased numbers needed for the planned wholesale gassing and burning of Hungary's Jews.

Afterwards the numbers were reduced, by the SS lie of a transfer to Gleiwitz of 200 from the special detail, loaded onto wagons, given food for the journey, then driven straight to a disinfection station. And gassed. The SS attempted to convince the special detail prisoners that their bodies were those of civilian workers killed in an Allied air raid. Not surprisingly they were disbelieved. Some of the bodies could be identified – and the SS had to do the burning during the night.

The advancing Red Army neared Majdanek. Nineteen Russians and a German kapo, transferred to the special unit at Auschwitz, made contact with Russian prisoners-of-war whose job in Birkenau was to dismantle aeroplanes. The Russians' help strengthened the resistors' determination to act for their freedom. This is where Roza and the explosive ingredient comes back into the story. Roza passed explosives on to a Russian technician called Borodin. He mixed that with other material and passed on cans of the mixture. The resistance movement let the special detail know that another round-up, euphemistically known as, transport to Gleiwitz, meaning, as before, death, was to take place. There was a general alarm – sparked into action by an unforeseen incident.

An SS guard beat up a Russian who tried to run off. The SS man fired at him. The man, though wounded, jumped from the wagon he was to be taken off in, snatched the whip from the SS man and hit him on the head. He was then killed. In some way this unexpected incident disrupted the timetable for the rebellion, which started prematurely. All that can be told of it has had to be pieced together, for there were no survivors.

Activists from the special detail had told Mikos Nyisli, a physician used for SS autopsies of the victims of medical experiments, that an uprising was planned for the evening of the 17th of October. To his surprise, at noon that day he heard an explosion, and shots. Lewental's buried account stated that the SS turned up at 1.25 p.m. to collect three hundred members of the detail. Knowing this meant death. rather than die tamely, they disobeyed the order to line up, rushed the guards, using hammers and axes, shouting, throwing stones. Under a hail of stones, overpowered SS men sustained serious wounds; some tried to run away. The crematorium burst into flames.

Although the action started sooner than planned, there is complete confirmation of Lewental's assertion that the crematorium was blown up and the fence cut. Some people got out, it is certain too that inmates at another crematorium disarmed their SS guards and killed them. Filip Müller heard that the Russians threw the chief kapo into the fire, greeted the SS with one of their home-made hand grenades, cut the wire with insulated pliers and ran out. Armed SS men quelled the uprising, some pursuing the escapees on motorbikes, while others overcame and shot anyone they found at the burning crematorium. Those who did escape hid in a barn at Rajkso, with the SS in pursuit. The SS set the barn on fire. All within perished. At the other two crematoria, petrol was hidden in readiness to set fire to the barracks but that part of their plan fell through, although the burned crematorium was quite unusable.

Three junior SS squad leaders were killed, twelve SS men wounded. From the roll numbers of prisoners, four hundred and fifty one prisoners perished. The political department's investigation to find out how the explosives got in led them to Roza, and three girls from the explosives factory. The usual tortures followed. Two of the smugglers, named by Martin Gilbert as Gisa Weissblum and Raiza Kibel, survived. At least three other Jewish girls as well as Roza, Ella Garnter, either Toszka or Estera Wajsblum and Regina Safir, are known to have been hanged.

A connecting thread between these prisoners held, in the unlikely shape of Jakob Kozelczuk. He had arrived with other Polish Jews in January 1943. Jakob's height and strength led to his being used as a bunker attendant, keeping the cellar cells in order, then leading condemned souls to the black wall where the public hangings took place. In due course he was appointed hangman. Those in the secret knew he courageously helped many prisoners. When Roza was held in the bunker, a friend of hers asked this Jakob to let him speak with her. Roza's friend had difficulty in recognising this was Roza, as she was after interrogation. But she was able to speak to him, assure him that the others involved in the smuggling had nothing to fear, she had only implicated a man she knew to be dead. She wrote some farewell words to her comrades. On January 6th, she and three other explosives smugglers were hanged in the women's camp.

Yet another thread in the story concerns young Kitty Felix, who, knowing nothing of the organisation though longing for something of the sort, had good reason, when she heard the explosion and saw the flames from the crematorium, to hope and believe that gold from the pile of dead victims' clothing, found as she searched it as part of her allocated work in the Kanada hut, gold she had taken great risks to pass on to the rumoured resistance movement, had indeed been used for bribery – bribery that helped obtain the smuggled explosives.

Jakob the hangman lived and though in Israel he was put on trial, many people came forward to testify on his behalf. He had put up with the role of hangman, and much opprobrium, in order to help wherever he could.

With the uprising put down, the secret recorders of such events decided that their testimony on what they had witnessed should be buried, in case their writers were murdered before the day of liberation. Salmen Gradowski chose to bury his account under the ashes. He reasoned rightly that after the defeat of Germany people would dig there to find the remains of millions of murdered people. Several such documents were recovered, still just legible.

Meanwhile, Wetzler and Vrba, seasoned by their time in the camp, had been appointed to work as block clerks. It took Julius Vrba some time to realise that the polite, helpful, gracious Ernst Burger, the clerk in Block 4, was in fact the acknowledged leader of the underground resistance movement; or to catch on to the fact that it was this movement that had helped him earlier on, before he even knew of its existence. Now, moving on from thoughts of personal freedom, he and Wetzler were both anxious to escape to tell what they knew, warn, alert, bring influences to bear, mitigate the dreadfulness. First they must discover the precise details of the extermination process.

Friends in the camp obtained documents. Filip Müller, the same prisoner who at that time worked in one of the special details, managed to remove the label from an emptied canister of Zyclon B gas. (Filip Müller survived Auschwitz, though once in desperation he'd tried to push himself in with people selected for the Zyclon B treatment. Whereupon the angry guards threw him out of the gas chamber, shouting that they were the ones who decided who was to die, and when. Systems. Rules. To be obeyed.)

The escape succeeded. Julius Vrba was hidden by Polish peasants. Reaching Slovakia he compiled a fifty-page report for the Jewish Council, describing in detail the camp's procedures, with statistics including the numbers of murdered people, based on notes he and Wetzler brought out of the camp.

What were these notes, how had Wetzler come by them? From prisoners working in the main office, and even in the political department, came little rolled-up pieces of paper, the numbers recorded on them all that was left to memorialise or dignify the lost lives: from Poland, from Germany, from France, from the occupied European countries, from non-occupied Slovakia. Before the escape on April 7th 1944, they reckoned, as a careful estimate, 1,750,000 Jews had been gassed. They were unable to give a similarly careful estimate of those others who had died from starvation, beatings, shootings, exhaustion or despair. Despair either of their own condition, of what they were reduced to, or despair of the human race, what its constituent peoples could bring themselves to do.

Additional information soon followed Wetzler and Vrba, when on May 27th, two more Jews, Arnost Rosin, Czeslaw Mordowicz, escaped from Birkenau. Reaching Slovakia, they met up with their two comrades and provided information on the round-up and murder of Hungarian Jews that had started in Birkenau eleven days previously. Nearly 400,000 Jews had been deported from Hungary to Auschwitz. From the post-war investigation it emerged Hitler had made it clear, he wanted 100,000 for the construction of six underground bombproof aeroplane factories. This top-priority selection, made at the loading platform at Birkenau, took from 15th of May till the 30th June. Coming from the Carpathian ghettos, these men were already half-starved when they arrived at the camp, yet, if the promises to Hitler made by his Hungarian stooges are to be believed, they were supposed to increase production in the underground sweat-shops by 40%, clearly an impossible task. Information on their situation added to the reports of Wetzler and Vbra, the completed documents and maps, were handed over to the Jewish Council and to the Papal Nuncio for Slovakia. A Polish major also escaped from Auschwitz with information. Detailed documentation from all three sources was passed on, in the July of 1944, to the Pope, to the governments of Great Britain and America and to the press. And the Papal Nuncio, the President of the International Committee of the Red Cross, the American Secretary of State, joined in to tell Admiral Horthy this was too much, they were aware that Jews were undoubtedly being liquidated at Auschwitz-Birkenau. At last the unbelievable, unbelieved information – so terrible that even some prisoners could not believe it – began to gain credence. With incalculable effects. On the orders of Miklos Horthy, the Regent in Hungary, units brought to Budapest to oversee more deportations were withdrawn. A loaded train already on its way to the camp was returned to its starting point. Horthy fell out of favour with Hitler, but that's another story.

Sketchy information on special detail attempts to escape their dreadful tasks indicates that as early as 1942 a foreman on the special detail night shift hoped to join with others in a mass breakout. That plan was betrayed, revealed to the SS either by men on barracks duty, or by the day shift foreman, who feared SS punishment if the plan succeeded. Three hundred more of the special detail were gassed after this, on 3rd December. Though little is known of similar rebellions, these were undoubtedly attempted, with at least one episode in July 1944 documented. Newly arrived Jews – who wouldn't know what they'd been let in for – were usually given the special detail job. Four hundred brought in from Cyprus had been in Birkenau camp for about three weeks, and they had found out. They all refused to work on the special details, and were themselves disposed of in the gas chambers – a memorable act of resistance in the face of overwhelming power.

In the later stages of the war, sabotage – where it could be carried out in such a way as not to exact the horrific reprisals Hitler ordered, that is, decimation, the shooting of every tenth inmate if there was even suspicion of sabotage – became an increasingly important element in the Combat Group's strategy. The German Armaments Works production mysteriously fell by half in a few months. At the Union Works, where a women's work detail was assigned, there were daily complaints that the grenades manufactured there failed to explode. Machines mysteriously broke down. After guns had passed inspection at the Rheinmetall Company, ingenious ways were found to damage the mechanism. At the Jawiszowice coal mine prisoners put rocks into the coal and wood supplies, they stole steel parts that were hard to obtain. Conveyor belts were damaged, fuel intended for locomotives was poured away into the crevices of rocks, mine timbers were thrown into inaccessible places. By April 11th 1944 sabotage had become a more serious crime than escape attempts. Camp commandants had orders, every member of a work detail proved to have taken part in sabotage should be publicly hanged. At this stage French prisoners such as Jules Frank were assisted to escape in anticipation of the camp's liberation. His success resulted in links between Frenchmen in the camp, a group of French prisoners of war and civilian workers nearby.

The Austrians and the Poles who headed up the Combat group had not confined themselves to practical activity, but kept up the argumentative side in talks and in written contributions to political debate. Consider Alfred Klahr, known for safety's sake by the name Lokmanis, who had been a member of the central committee of the Austrian Communist Party. In Auschwitz he wrote a detailed theoretical study of the German question, including a discussion of the shared responsibility of the German people for the crimes of National Socialism and indicating the need for the working class people in Germany to overcome the effects of Fascist ideology on their thinking, calling on the German Communist Party members to re-consider their own attitudes in this respect. (Klahr-Lokmanis would later take part in an escape attempt, which would link him up with the Polish partisans, and he got as far as Warsaw before the Gestapo killed him.) The Combat Group kept up its information seeking and sending. A letter dated 25th March 1944 passed details to the Polish underground about Katowice airport, and hospitals nearby.

By September of that year, the defeats of the German armies on the Eastern Front would lead to Hitler's orders to Himmler: wipe out all signs of the camps. The Combat Group rightly feared the SS intention to destroy all evidence, buildings and people alike; in the basement room of Block 4 Ernst Burger reported he'd made contact with a Russian resistance group – and proposed re-organising their forces in preparation for an armed rebellion in co-operation with the partisans. Instead of their previous policy of eyes and ears everywhere, they would place their people in the motor pool, the clothing depot and, to get at weapons, the troops' quarters; put more comrades working outside the chain of checkpoints; and set up a military leadership, solely concerned with planning rebellion. Other Polish-led groups would collaborate.

A detailed plan for co-ordination with outside resistance forces, assessment of the SS forces' equipment and weapons, the location of weapon stores and alarm systems, as well as estimates of the numbers of prisoners who, once freed, would fight with the Allied forces, was sent to groups of Polish partisans who met to discuss what could be done, and how to overcome the difficulty of hiding and providing for large numbers of escaped ex-prisoners. Then the Polish government-in-exile had an officer parachuted in, who went by the code name of Urban. Urban was captured. Perhaps not the most experienced of agents, he had the plans for the actions to liberate the camp on him. The Germans sent him there as a prisoner, as the Combat Group soon informed their Cracow contacts.

Transfers of many active resistors followed this debacle. The leaders of the Combat Group, though not betrayed, had their forces severely weakened by the transfers. An open rebellion ceased to be a practical possibility. The fear of everyone's death hung over them.

The next decision of Combat Group Auschwitz involved sending out two Austrians, together with two Poles, to join with the local Polish partisans, doing their utmost to prevent the deaths of all at the camp before the Red Army's approach would free them. Prepared hiding places in the chain of guard stations concealed the chosen men for three nights. Then they were sneaked out to a pre-arranged spot. Alfred Klahr and Stefan Bratkowski got out first, then six more dribbled out too. For the escape of the executive committee, different methods had to be employed. An SS uniform and a pass were obtained. Hermann Langbein produced a cover story that required him to map all the swamps where malaria bred, so that these could be treated to prevent an epidemic. Escorted by guards, he was allowed to scout the route, map in hand, to the spot where the partisans would meet them with clothes and weapons. A day before the date decided on, the Group was informed that the partisans had problems; the attempt must be postponed. Moreover, Langbein's foray had attracted attention; he was transferred to a sub-camp of Neuengamme.

The Group waited until October 27th before trying again. Two SS were bribed to drive five members of the Combat Group's executive out of the camp in a box supposedly containing dirty laundry. One SS man betrayed them. The partisan group was ambushed at the agreed meeting place. The escape vehicle was driven, not to meet the partisans, but to the bunker. The five had been prepared for failure, they swallowed poison. Two died, the others had stomach pumps used on them and had to endure torture. They did not betray anyone. With two Austrians who had conducted the negotiations with the SS, they were hanged. Publicly, in the roll-call area. One of them was Ernst Burger, whose role in the camp had been so outstanding.

Outside contacts were however informed of the urgent need to stop the SS plan to destroy the camp and all within it. Broadcasts from Britain warned of severe punishments that would be handed out by the Allies to anyone involved. The SS abandoned the destruction plan, but evacuation marches resulted in terrible loss of prisoners' lives, all the more bitter as this was so near to the end of the war. The orders received from Himmler on 17th January 1945 had been for total evacuation, away from the approaching Soviet army. 60,000 prisoners were herded out, marched off in the snow, to camps further east; if they got there. Those who did, kept up the struggle to live, and some even found friendly help. A few men, women and children remained in the camp infirmary, where the doctors kept their heads, chance somehow exempting them from the evacuation death marches. The Red Army liberated the camp on January 27th. About 7,000 sick and exhausted prisoners – about 4,000 of them women – remained there alive, compared with the last roll-call numbers of 31,894, of whom 16,577 were women. The last known number to have been tattooed on a male prisoner was 202,499.

An account of being marched away, together with her mother, has been given by Danielle Raphael, who wrote under her later name of Eva Brewster. Warned by a friend from the camp, Otto, she stole warm clothing for herself and her women friends, who were to be marched off, fast, over snow-covered mountains. Otto advised her, they must not drop to the back of the march, nor should they be at the side, within reach of blows from the guards. They must keep to the middle, they must keep up. He had brought boots for Danielle and her mother, they must wear them straight away, so they would be worn in before they were put to the test on the forced march.

It was January 25th. Lined up in the snow, marched off, they walked all day without food or rest, sleeping that night in an abandoned barn where bales of straw gave some warmth. At dawn, with snow for breakfast, they were off again. Women who'd worked in the laundry department were in good health, and due to their mutual support system, relatively well fed. During the night, some discussed chancing an escape; but Danielle had been warned by Otto to wait until they were out of Poland.

Through deep forests that day, many falling behind, their feet swollen and bleeding, the guards hysterical in their fear of attack by partisans. The night spent in an open field. It was here that Danielle's mother Elisabeth, not for the first time, saved her daughter's life. This woman of iron determination told everyone they must keep awake, keep moving. Many were too tired to take notice. When Danielle too would have dropped asleep in the snow, her mother grabbed her by the wrist, made her walk about, keep awake, run the length of the field. Those who survived that freezing night must keep on again all the next day. At last they were loaded onto the open wagons of a coal truck. As they jolted along, Elisabeth recognised their surroundings, they were near to Kattowitz, an area she knew well. Mother and daughter made a spur-of-the-moment escape, jumping from the train with the help of Susan, one of their friends from the camp. Eventually Danielle and Elisabeth reached good friends in Berlin and a reasonably safe place until, the war over, the number 5149 tattooed onto Danielle's arm no longer must be hidden from the sight of those Nazi-minded Germans who might still have them sent to their deaths. Of the thousand or so who had been in the evacuation contingent with them, those who stayed on the train on its way to Bergen-Belsen? Only five besides themselves known to have survived.

By chance another mother and her daughter Kitty Felix also survived Auschwitz and the deadly march away. Kitty and her mother, after a year and a half of unexpected survival – toughened by their pre-camp initiation into a hard life under the Nazi regime, kept alive by helping each other, receiving and giving help to those they came across – and by Kitty's work assignment in the 'Kanada' detail, were selected for a move, in November of 1944.

Kitty stole warm clothes; bread was issued, a train of cattle trucks stood ready at the siding. Bolted inside, crowded together in pitch darkness, they waited – would the jolting train take them to the crematorium, or to another camp? It was to Gross-Rosen camp, in use now as a transit camp, after one night travelling on, reaching a small camp near the Telefunken factory. At first the German workers in the factory seemed afraid even to look at these new labourers. The SS women guards patrolled, making sure no contacts took place. After a while, when Kitty suffered a badly burned arm which the SS refused to have treated, the German woman working next to her began to show sympathy, even hiding a sandwich for her and smiling when the SS woman was not watching. Kitty shared the daily sandwich with her mother, they all scrounged or stole to survive the winter's cold. An air of friendship pervaded this hut of assorted women.

By February 1945 when distant gunfire began to be heard, heralding the approach of Soviet troops, another move was ordered. The only route open was to the west, across a mountain pass. Thousands were assembled, Kitty and her mother huddling together with their group of friends. February 18th, dawn just breaking over the Eulengebirge mountain range. Slowly moving on, women from Kitty's group began to lag behind, helped on, some carried, by their friends. They tried to admire the mountain range in sunshine, or distract each other from their misery by talking – and singing. Another night on the mountainside without shelter. Many died. Once over the summit, they were in farmland. They stole whatever food they could get their hands on. The columns kept going, their numbers lessening. For two days, a pause at Trautenau camp, foraging for food in the general disorder.

One hundred of Kitty's group had left Auschwitz together, and at that stage were still alive, although the 10,000 or so who had been marched on from their last working camp had shrunk nearly to 2,000. Now another train journey, this time in open coal trucks. Backwards and forwards, round in circles, travelling for five days, near to the Dutch border, but still in Germany, arriving at a camp run by Dutch women who not only had never heard of gas chambers, they found it impossible to believe in such devices. Kitty and friends were marched to work in an underground factory (owned by Philips), on fourteen-hour shifts. Her mother, based at the camp, organised hot soup for her daughter, and hot water so she could wash properly. Air raids, at first frequent, became continuous. While the Dutch prisoners excitedly awaited liberation, the fears of the old hands from Auschwitz, that the evacuation rows of five would once again be assembled, proved only too well-founded. Fourteen out of that 100 were entrained that day. The rest of the group, and thousands of others taken to the forest nearby - machine-gunned.

At Fallersleben a short stay, no work but little food available. Then on again, in cattle trucks, headed for Bergen-Belsen, that place of dread already so overcrowded they were refused admission; long trainloads filled with locked-in prisoners were lined up on the tracks. Forced into a truck by armed guards and their dogs, the doors locked and nailed up, the only air trickled in from a crack in the floorboards that Kitty enlarged with a penknife, nearly suffocating when two SS men heard their calls for help and opened the truck, but with no idea what to do; after talking things over, one of them decided to go to a camp he knew of, and ask if they had room there for the women. This small camp outside Salzwezel admitted them, after the extra march to get there, to what now seemed desirable shelter.

But by April 13th all were near starvation. Scribbled notes fluttered over the camp, warnings from a group of French prisoners; the Germans were planning to blow up the camp, but prisoners would try to cut off the electric current so escape would be less dangerous. At last only one solitary SS man was seen. The women attacked him. Kitty took his dagger. A military convoy approached, its soldiers wearing American uniforms. At the shouts of the women, two tanks turned towards them. Their liberation had begun.

The two young Jewish women, Danielle and Kitty – though the first came from an old-established German family and the second was Polish – have in their stories elements in common. Both their mothers were above the age allowed for survival for work-purposes on entry to the camp where work was supposed to make them free. Neither of the daughters could have survived without the strength of their mothers in helping them, their own determination to be of help to their mothers, the help given by women who formed with them a friendship group, almost a family. Post-liberation, came a moment of temptation to an act of revenge on German persons. Danielle, now free, chose not to shoot an SS woman whose cruelty had been manifested in the camp; Kitty realised, if she used her dagger to kill an ordinary family of Germans now cowering before her, the nazis would have succeeded.

Neither woman had played active parts in a resistance movement they barely guessed at within Auschwitz-Birkenau. Nevertheless the accounts they wrote and the lives they lived afterwards were, for both, motivated by the strong desire to counter seeds of prejudice, intolerance or the selfish unhelpfulness of complacency they found in their new environments. They wrote their stories filled with the need to warn, to inform. Many years later, surviving 'hidden children', encouraged at last to relate their experiences, expressed similar responses, their wish for the future, for their children's future, for all our futures.

BUCHENWALD – DORA

On the 11th August 1938 a Reuters despatch came to the attention of 'The Manchester Guardian'. This paper then reported that the German general public were well aware, that 'everyone' in Weimar knew of Buchenwald camp and its location, 'but nobody mentions the dreaded words, concentration camp'. This report was confirmed by a message to the Foreign Office from its Berlin Embassy, which added that relatives were required to pay three marks to collect the ashes of relatives who had died there.

Buchenwald had begun its notorious career, holding Germans, fewer than 8,000, before September 1938. The first senior camp officials appointed from among these were brutal criminals. 20,000 additional prisoners followed from the events on Kristallnacht, on November 9th to November 10th, when windows of Jewish homes and Jewish-owned shops were smashed, the owners killed, beaten up, or sent to Buchenwald, others to Dachau and Orianenberg, their fate reported by British and American journalists.

Three processes pushed numbers down again, to about 5,400. Before the war criminals and those with only a short sentence were released after serving their time, or to celebrate Hitler's birthday. Others were transferred. Jews would be released if they were ransomed and could emigrate. But the most commonly used departure method was named by the Nazis as, departure by death.

Yet in 1938 a criminal prisoner tried to escape, killing an SS man during his attempt. Re-captured, returned to the camp, sentenced to public hanging, a German political prisoner, Fritz Männchen, was ordered to act as hangman – an order he refused to carry out.

Seven hundred Germans who arrived in September 1939 formed a communist party branch. Led by Harry Kuhn and Albert Kuntz they welded together a tightly organised group of resistors, with radios tuned to news broadcasts from foreign stations. As more prisoners from more countries of origin arrived they added their skills; Germans, Austrians. Poles, Czechs, Dutchmen, linking up resistance groups and ridding themselves of criminal kapos and informers. For while not every green kapo was brutal, not every red kapo kind, overall, changes in relative strengths within the camp could mean the difference between death and life. Among the worst treated were homosexuals. Nation-wide arrests of homosexual men followed the setting up of a 'special department' on both abortion and homosexuality on October 26th, 1934. At first placed among the political prisoners, then in 1938 collected up and sent to the penal section, on killingly hard work in a quarry, unable to gain armbands, regarded warily by the resistance in case they'd been prevailed on to act as informers, few in numbers, disunited, they were undeservedly stigmatised, there and elsewhere.

The laundry and the storage rooms saw the first red armband wearers. Then the hospital staff acquired able men – a core of 'red' prisoners who had been held since 1933. Their organisational skills had developed, as had their ingenuity. Forming first in groups of three or five, nineteen regional groups came together, a community, comradeship its keynote, discipline, preparedness and experience its means of not getting caught.

Pre-war, even Ernst Platz, a social-democratic journalist from Berlin sent to Buchenwald in the spring of 1938, came into the possible release category. The German communists placed him under their protection and admitted him to secret meetings, in return for his promise – if released, he would tell the world about Buchenwald. The comrades took only five days to get him moved from the penal colony for incoming Jews. For thirteen months he obeyed instructions to train his memory prior to his release. This was one of the earliest episodes of planned schemes for sending out information.

The committee's policy of protecting the lives of endangered prisoners had been decided early on in the history of this camp. Such men as the communist Ernst Busse, who had been a Reichstag member, brought experience and attitudes that would play a well-remembered part, as did Robert Siewert and Otto Horn. Siewert particularly stressed the need to aid weak or sick people, to organise a fair distribution of food, to espouse as a main aim, mutual help to all. Busse added to this the need to form effective fighting groups to safeguard prisoners' lives and to gain their freedom, in the perilous situations he rightly anticipated when the Nazi regime would collapse.

Packages from relatives were allowed in; the 'politicals' arranged for fair distribution (despite thieving by the criminal elements). Then when agreement was reached that some contents could be held back for the purpose of bribing the highly corruptible SS guards, who to bribe with what, and for which purpose, developed into a specialist skill. Karl Barthel, appointed as senior camp inmate, took advantage of his privileged position in the SS officers' mess to write accounts of the camp, compiled from information passed on by Czech prisoners. German civilians, with the connivance of two SS group leaders, sent this written evidence out to Barthel's wife. By the summer of 1942, the German-led groups gained strength, first from the Russian prisoners-of-war sent there, then from Russian civilians. More Czechs, Spanish, Italian, Yugoslavs and Poles arrived. By 1943, an international camp committee formed on the initiative of the many German communists such as Walter Bartel. A military-style organisation co-operated with the communist leadership, a smaller Polish group of communists worked in the hospital, all known about from details enshrined in the literature of the camps. A popular-front committee formed in February 1944 on the initiative of the social democrat official Hermann Brill. This set out a joint agreement on what the prisoners decided on as a just set of policies, to be worked for when the war was over.

Two camp doctors behaved both well and badly. Dr. Hoven confounds judgement, his behaviour full of contrasts. What can one say about a doctor who on the one hand took part, with no apparent distaste, in giving lethal injections or experimenting with typhus, and on the other sought medical improvements and better hygiene, took care of individual patients and openly helped the political prisoners in their efforts to curb criminals? It seems that money brought into the camp after Kristallnacht had its effect on Dr. Hoven. He then served two masters. Intellectually too, he showed some reliance on prisoners; his doctoral dissertation was written by the Austrian communist Gustav Wegerer and the Czech physicist Kurt Sitte. No wonder he helped the politicals to stop the activities of dangerous informers, and to his credit he saved many resistance people from execution.

Dr Erwin Ding-Schuler changed under the influence of his clerk, Eugen Kogan.

Buchenwald's department of typhus and viral research turned into a haven for political prisoners, some sixty-five of them employed in Block 50, sheltering there – with Ding-Schuler's knowledge – from an execution threat. Yet in the early days of the camp, before he was found to be so easily corruptible that he would sell the prisoners anything, even, it is said, his pistol, he is known to have been a murderer.

Eugen Kogan is, however, unequivocal about one medical officer, August Feld. This man had his eyes opened when he was assigned, in 1941, to the so-called hygienics institute. After seeing for himself what happened there he did not need convincing that he should take risks to help the prisoners. On one memorable occasion, he escorted a Dutch prisoner, Jan Robert, on a trip to Jena. The prisoner's task, ostensibly, was to examine specialised books on typhus at the University. In reality Feld visited Kogan's family for him while Robert carried out tasks set by the resistance group. Feld, and also an elderly medical officer called Rose, who gave to the best of his ability what help he could, seem like lights in that dark night. Not only for what they did, but for the contrast between their actions and those of other qualified doctors known to have conducted vile experiments and mass murders which they 'justified' on the appalling grounds of their 'subjects' sub-humanity.

Radio receivers, despite regulations and decrees, continued to be built, hidden – a group from Pilsen hid one they had made in a petrol drum – and avidly listened to. The Russians concealed their radio, made with the help of a Polish radio engineer, Gwidon Damazyn, under the false bottom of a shoe polish bucket. In three and a half years, Damazyn, working at night, constructed seven more radios with parts smuggled in from the Garrison Administration, where Damazyn's specialist qualifications were thought by the SS to be used solely on their behalf. Damazyn and other electrical experts went on constructing throughout their time in the camp. This had important results before the end. Who knows how important?

The camp commandant was so corrupt that even he could not get away with it; in 1942 he was sacked and replaced by a less depraved commandant, Pister, who gave jobs to the politicals rather than to the criminals. The rate of executions decreased, and in spite of problems arising from overcrowding and epidemics, by August of 1943 the death rate had dropped dramatically. Pister even agreed to let the prisoners form their own Camp Defence committee, and by this means they were able to put a stop to the beatings with which newcomers were routinely greeted by SS guards.

There is a saying, attributed to Polish women prisoners: 'sabotage is like wine'. The Buchenwald contingents, unwillingly roped in for war work, were not backward in coming forward in this sphere of activity. A Russian, Yuri Sapunov, received instructions from the camp committee to organise work in such a way that although as little as possible got done, no trouble resulted either from going slow or from the frequent mysterious breakdowns of equipment. Another Russian, the physicist Alexei Gurin, was assigned the task of organising sabotage in the sub-camp Schwerte, where locomotive repair work was done. The construction of the Gustloff Works provided another resounding field of action for Buchenwald saboteurs who ingeniously delayed its completion by several months. Enormous quantities of cement were wasted as the foundations were laid, and by Siewert's account shafts for hydraulic elevators and lifts, a big montage shaft for missiles, and the test range, were never made watertight. A great number of interference elements got built in to the connections to the power lines, neatly disrupting the power supply.

When the plant did get going, among the 6,000 prisoner-workers placed there were anti-Nazis of all nationalities, people of such calibre that they could be relied on to take risks to hinder the Nazi war effort. The methods used included over-ordering the machines, the tools, the materials required for a given job, as well as ordering, over many months, supplies for a long-abandoned production project, of course accidentally (the Good Soldier Schweik would have liked that one). Prisoners turned to good account the passion of the Wehrmacht for rules and regulations governing each and every last detail of inspection and purchase. By fostering disputes among the bureaucracy in charge of the management structure and by carrying out the Wehrmacht's finicky requirements to the letter and past it, they were able to delay the passing of many items with minor, unimportant flaws – while components which had major defects sailed through the inspection procedures. Russian specialists such as Anatoly Skobtsov had this method so well worked out that on one occasion the Wehrmacht sent back nine months production of automatic carbines, all of which were unserviceable, though the cause of this was not only not obvious, it proved to be undetectable.

During 1944, an especially urgent war order came in. What could be done to delay it? The doctors played their part, informing the commandant they had diagnosed a typhus outbreak in workers at the plant. Terrified of the spread of this mythical outbreak to civilian workers, the commandant responded with a quarantine order, which delayed for two weeks those urgently wanted parts. Sabotage efforts intensified after the arrival of a contingent of French metalworkers, the low level of technical and organisational know-how of non-prisoner foremen and engineers meant that they were often dependent on the abilities of prisoner-workmen, who had the skills but no intention of using them on the Nazi's behalf if ways round the situation could be found. As a result, production figures failed to match up with the amount of machinery available. Machines adequate for making 15,000 carbine barrels a month – the production target was 10,000 – after eighteen months only turned out a maximum of 8,000. Even producing that reduced quantity had required four to ten times as many expensive tools as were stipulated.

The authorities became suspicious. An investigating committee sent to see what went on was interrupted by Allied air raids which almost destroyed the Gustloff Works, as well as the German Armaments Works and other military installations. Since not all the machinery had been damaged, prisoners obligingly helped during their stints clearing up in the toolhouse, putting out of commission as many undamaged expensive machine tools as they could get at.

Meanwhile, a momentous event in the August of 1943; the opening of a subsidiary camp, Dora. (This later became a camp with satellite camps, but continuing administrative links with Buchenwald proved useful for information and sabotage purposes.) Prisoners from Buchenwald transferred to work at Dora learned its great secret. The tides of war were to be turned, so the Nazis thought, through the use of a new miracle weapon. This device had in fact been the subject of much earlier research, its rocket engines exploiting a loophole in the post 1914-1918 war settlement. Werner Von Braun headed the research team testing rockets at Peenemunde. Though Hitler was apparently not impressed by the test he witnessed there, the fledgling weapon did travel at four times the speed of sound, so would be formidable if it could be developed. Its research team is said not to have thought of it as a weapon but as a research project. The Luftwaffe proposed making it into a 'flying bomb', working on a 'pulse jet' system, and the FI103 became the prototype for Cruise missiles. By 1943, when British Intelligence had evidence for rocket building at the first site at Peenemunde, bombing raids caused considerable damage there. The Nazis searched for a secure site. V1 and particularly V2 weapons were highly effective, causing vast damage on London, with huge civilian casualties and fear of the 'doodlebug' weapons. In the case of V2s they could not be heard approaching nor could they be intercepted. On hearing that this new and frightful weapon was to be built at Dora, in specially constructed underground tunnels deep in the mountainside, the Buchenwald comrades assigned its most dependable and experienced people to work there. Six German communists and one social democrat were soon followed by four more communists and two from the German Socialist party. The Frenchman Claude Louth, despite better working conditions available to him in his open air job, volunteered for a detail working on the production of the 'miracle' weapons, so that he too would be in a favourable position to take part in their sabotage.

At first the prisoners were not allowed to leave the tunnels. That did not stop sabotage or efforts to get information out about production of the rockets. Expert workers, with the help of those in key positions, were steered to work where their knowledge could be put to use disabling the missiles. Albert Kuntz, who headed the construction office, convinced the commandant Fröschner and the director of Sawatzk Works that political prisoners would be more useful than greens in running the camp, thus replacing criminal kapos. A Czech doctor, Jan Cespiva, who regarded himself as chief dispatcher of saboteurs, moved them from the hospital to tasks in appropriate places. So electrical engineers were assigned to work on the steering device in the tail of the missile, their instructions to change the voltage in the relays of the receivers. Another underground hero, a Pole, Jozef Radzyminski, one of the Spanish War veterans, and a communist, has been written of by Krokowski as being one of the finest fellows in Dora, despite Krokowski's opposition to the Pole's political views. Sabotage came both from planned interference with the production schedule and individual initiatives in stealing useful things or damaging parts. The Russians' method was very direct, they urinated on transformers and other parts, and disrupted the power supply by cutting cables. A Frenchman and a Pole collaborated to add a powder to the oil used for the missiles.

The combined results of independent actions and organised obstruction are shown in recorded statistics. From the night of June 15th to 16th 1944, of some 11,300 V1 rockets targeted at England, about one-fifth failed. V2 rocket firing began in September; between then and the following March, only about half of the 10,800 firings reached their target area. 5,000 either fell into the sea, exploded, or fell apart in the starting area. Not all these failures were due to sabotage – the techniques needed for making such novel weapons had to be tested and corrected. Nonetheless, the authorities thought sabotage and stealing of parts were of sufficient importance for a network of spies and informers to be set up. Many arrests followed. Effects for the prisoners from the deaths of the strongest of their resistance people, would be harmful indeed, in the latter days of the camp.

Information on Dora's products must be smuggled out. Some letters, heavily censored, were permitted, so Breton prisoners used words in their letters that the German censors would not understand and consequently might mistake for a person's name. A nod being as good as a wink, someone might gain an inkling of what was hinted at in the strangely-worded letter just arrived from Dora. And if prisoners were transferred to other camps, someone there might be able to send word out. A Polish physician sent out a letter, its details written in invisible ink, safely received by a friend who knew how to look for the secret message. Even when Dora's status changed from that of a subsidiary of Buchenwald to that of a separate camp, links with the Buchenwald troublemakers were maintained.

Franz Fox, a 'green' kapo who worked in the crematorium at Dora, is an example of a well-disposed criminal. It had come to the ears of the SS that the prisoners planned to make a radio transmitter. This information came in its turn to the ears of the prisoners involved. Putting their trust in Fox, they asked him to destroy the parts they had for it, before a search could take place. Fox was willing to help out, but this too became known to the SS. Searching the crematorium, they found the hidden transmitter components. What happened next is known, for it so happened that a Polish prisoner shared the cell that Fox was shut up in, in the bunker. That man reported, that all Fox would say to the SS was, he was not a communist, he didn't concern himself with politics, he was an old professional criminal – and the word betrayal wasn't in his vocabulary.

Eugen Kogan, the clerk to the camp doctor, took part in the web of intrigue that smuggled out news of Dora. He telephoned it out, using the doctor's telephone and telling the operator he was the doctor. He was believed, so he called a police station at Unna. There a friend of his friend Heinz Baumeister, a fellow social-democrat, was a civil defence officer. He told Baumeister – not of course using his own name, but a pre-arranged pseudonym – that the blueprints of the subterranean buildings at Dora, stored in the hygienics institute of Buchenwald where Kogan could get at them, would be hidden in a book jacket and sent to him.

The political stance of communists, socialists and social-democrats, though important for organised action, was by no means the only basis for the rejection of Nazi notions. Religious belief endowed some men and women with heroic strengths. For instance, Frère Birin, who had it whispered to him in Buchenwald that it would not be wise to identify himself as a clergyman, was allocated work in Dora instead of being sent to Dachau. Birin's moral strength resulted in his being held in high regard. Christian as well as Jewish religious practice was Verboten, strictly Verboten too. But the tunnels of Dora, like to the catacombs of Roman times, came in useful as a venue for secretly held services; the making of Eucharist wafers, unlikely as it sounds, a part of this endeavour.

A particularly strong German protestant pastor, Paul Schneider, held in the cells near the roll call area, shouted his sermons through the bars of the window. Slapped down by the guards before he'd got out more than a sentence or two, he nevertheless kept on shouting out his sermon. The effect of this man's fearlessness on the long ranks of prisoners assembled for the roll call would long last within them, after Paul Schneider was killed by the SS.

The German Jewish communist Rudi Arndt, who became senior block inmate, made enormous efforts to give encouragement to all those who could write poems or songs, as manifestations of true humanity alive in Buchenwald. A string quartet played Mozart, Haydn, Beethoven – moments of relief, of mental release, of a chance for essential inner reserves of strength to be mustered from those concerts. Reserves of strength were activated too by the courage of individuals such as the senior camp inmate, Georg Thomas. When two escapees were captured and brought back to Dora, in the February of 1944, the prisoners were assembled in the roll-call area for the paraphernalia attendant on a public hanging. The order was given for Thomas to hang them. In a voice loud enough for all to hear, he called out, 'I refuse to carry out this order!' The same order, given to the deputy senior inmate Ludwig Szymczak, met with the same reply. Eventually a German criminal did hang the re-captured men. Thomas and Szymczak were both put in the bunker for a while then let back into camp jobs, though no longer as senior inmates.

Saving an individual's life through the swapping-numbers game, though risky, became a well-thought out and organised method, with tattooed numbers replaced at night, the live man saved through identity-exchange with a dead man; perhaps dozens, in the course of time perhaps as many as a hundred and thirty, re-numbered, re-named, and sent on a transport to another camp to obviate the risk of an informer recognising him if he stayed in the same camp. Patients in the hospital could sometimes be saved by a method devised by infirmary kapo Ernst Busse. Prisoners wanted by the Gestapo, or those about to be transferred to a worse camp, were declared unfit for transport. After an American air raid destroyed documents kept by the administration's political department, many endangered inmates were re-listed under false names, and Jews re-described as Aryan.

Unusually, a group of thirty seven French, Belgian and Canadians officers, who turned out to be captured agents of the Allied secret services, arrived at the camp soon after the bombing of the Gustloff Works. A few days later, sixteen of the newcomers were lined up and killed. Eugen Kogan and Heinz Baumeister decided on a personal intervention to save the lives of the rest of the agents. Three of them who spoke French were placed in the infirmary to replace dead Frenchmen. One was given a high temperature from a milk injection, and a tipsy SS chief squad leader, fooled into thinking he was at death's door anyway, reported him dead. Then an opportunity arose to change the identity of others.

The camp resistance increased its efforts to obtain weapons. The military command, preparing for action when the time should be ripe, had in August 1943 hidden ten guns from Gustloff, in places as varied as the coke depot of the corpse incinerator chamber, the medicine cellar of the hospital and the bath. Then when SS men were sent from an SS penal camp to Buchenwald, a purchase from them of arms in exchange for margarine (supplied by the canteen kapo Heinz Schafer) was organised by Kurt Leeser. The pistols he got hold of were hidden in the SS hospital, where Leeser worked as a pharmacist. Franz Bera, one of the Austrian communists, took advantage of the difficulty the SS now had in keeping close control of everything. As well as acquiring pistols, hand grenades, and ammunition he held sessions on how to use them, in the pathology section where Gustav Wegerer was kapo.

Instructions on their duties had been given to the medical corps sent in to Gustloff after air raids there. In addition to bandaging the wounded and recovering the dead, they were told by the resistance to salvage military material, including the pistols and bayonets of dead SS men. A group of special prisoners, Norwegian students, joined in. For training in the use of weapons, marksmanship, and in the use of bazookas, the military skills of Russian prisoners of war, of members of the French maquis, Yugoslav partisans, Spaniards and German or Austrian veterans of the Spanish civil war, and former Polish and Czech soldiers, were invoked. Lessons in topography and tactics formed part of their preparations.

Escapes would usually be planned and effected with the help of a group, or at least several sympathetic friends. A bizarre escape took place in 1944. It was early June. An outside detail working at Arolsen included the Belgian Fernand Labalue, the Pole Adolf Korzynski, and two from Luxembourg, Pierre Schaul and Nicolas Wolff. All were young. The combination of their positions in the camp was favourable: the automobile shop, the clothing depot, the SS barber department. Schaul the Barber stole the SS keys and got copies made. Labalue took SS uniforms from the clothing store. Korzynski and Wolff repaired a broken-down car that stood abandoned in the garage. One Sunday morning Korzynski, the oldest one, donned the uniform of a general. The others had to be content with uniforms of lower rank. They had acquired road maps, and a compass. They could produce their orders for a courier trip to Saarbrucken. They got in the car. Drove to the gate. The guard did what was required of him, he gave them a military salute. They drove on, going west, until they ran out of petrol. They hid the car, then went on, on foot. It was a long way to walk, they were crossing half Germany. They boarded a train, its destination Trier. They split up to avoid the controls at the station, and getting into Luxembourg after ten days of travelling, they reached friends, exchanged the uniforms for civilian clothes, and dropped out of sight, though their exploit was recorded in a Luxembourg newspaper, complete with photographs.

At the camp the stock of arms stolen, smuggled, haggled for, or made in workshops and secretly stored, rose to ninety-one carbines and 2,500 bullets, one light machine gun, 2,000 bullets, (opportunistically stolen when an SS man had forgotten he'd left his gun in an escort vehicle that prisoners must unload) twenty small firearms, 200 Molotov cocktails made with chemicals smuggled in from the German Armaments Works and the SS pharmacy, cutting and stabbing weapons, hand grenades made by camp chemists and Russian prisoners; and after the bombing that burned down the SS arsenal, five pistols filched and repaired by Franz Bera, and tested on the SS rifle range in the basement. Dora, too, had its collection of hand grenades, explosives – and poisons.

These weapons, originally symbols of the power that kept them imprisoned half-way between life and death, passed to the prisoners a segment of that power – but power to be used for worthwhile purposes, a means of protecting themselves and their fellow-inmates, when the most dangerous though most hopeful moment came, the moment when Allied forces drew near, the moment of desperation and fear in the Nazi hierarchy, which would most surely order their complete destruction.

The military committee had prepared two plans, Plan A, Plan B. Plan A involved taking the offensive to liberate themselves, hardly a practical proposition at that moment. Plan B was a strategy for their protection.

But before Allied forces reached Dora the network of informers within the camp had betrayed the resistance group. Its members were arrested and killed, the worker-prisoners closely guarded by a contingent of criminal prisoners armed by the SS. When evacuations began on April 4th, without the seasoned characters of the resistance organisation there was no chance of stopping or even influencing the chaotic way this was pushed through. For those left behind at Dora there was no food, no hospital care, no assurance that rescuers would come before all were dead.

At the main Buchenwald camp the knowledge of what evacuation would mean for its prisoners had been made crystal clear with the arrival of the exhausted remnant, less than half of the number who'd set out, of a large group of prisoners marched away from Auschwitz. The ones who didn't make it had either dropped by the roadside, were shot if they fell behind, or, packed into sealed cattle cars, arrived weeks later, already dead.

American troops were still not near enough to Buchenwald for any hope of immediate help if a rebellion were started, and the prisoners lacked the forces to succeed without such help. That was the opinion of the German comrades, who were reluctant to risk the lives of the 80,000 or so prisoners held in Buchenwald and its various satellite camps, although the Russians had in the December of 1944 put forward a plan, with French and Czech support, asking the international committee to set a definite date for an armed uprising. It took until February 1945 for the groups to work out a concerted plan to delay evacuation of the camp, if the order for this should come. In this plan the camp was divided and sub-divided into combat zones and sectors. Three stages of alert provided the basis for training up the resistance groups. Maps, drawn to a scale of 1 to 25,000, were distributed to key members. The French communist section's leaders continued urging the international political and military organisations to take action as soon as conditions permitted.

The expected evacuation began with the transport of 1,500 to Theresienstadt on April 3rd. On April 4th all Jews were ordered to come forward. This was the trigger for open resistance. Except for a few who decided to turn up, the Jews did not show in the roll call area. Instead of the SS dragging them from their barracks by force, they ordered all the senior block inmates to identify and report the Jews in the various barracks; most had already ripped off the yellow Star of David from their clothing. Next morning the Jews still did not turn up at roll call. The senior block inmates reported they had been unable to carry out the order to produce them. Twenty SS men, heavily armed, were sent to examine each prisoner's racial status, segregating those they identified as Jews. Block by block, building by building, they searched the camp, eventually isolating about 1,500 of the 6,000. These were placed under heavy guard, though some slipped out and away, helped by the Camp Defence to merge into the ranks of the other prisoners. On the following day Hungarian Jews arriving from Ohrdruf were added to the numbers.

On the evening of April 5th the camp administration decided the transport was complete – only partial victory for the sabotage attempt, but two days of delay represented a real international effort by the camp resistance to save their Jewish comrades. And the inevitable repercussions followed; the commandant gave the clerks a list of forty-six prisoners ordered to line up by the gate on the following morning. This list included German, Dutchmen, Poles, Czechs, Austrians and Frenchmen, two German and one Austrian Jew, people in key positions, clearly suspected by the camp administration. Fortunately, they'd had eight hours warning; Dr. Ding-Schuler told Eugen Kogan, in confidence, that the list had been compiled so that key personnel could be executed before they could block the next evacuation order. The internal camp organisation met at night, discussing the possibility of an armed uprising. The military situation had not yet turned in their favour. They decided the forty-six would be hidden within the camp, with this proviso, that if the SS tried to drag one man of them to the gate by force, force would be used against them. The news was spread throughout the camp. The international camp committee, whose spokesmen made the announcement that night in each of the blocks, was, for the first time, openly spoken of to the thousands who knew nothing (though some suspected) of a secret organisation. Next morning the stooges of the 'Camp Defence' were ordered to search for them, find the missing men, on pain of death if they were not found; but found they were not.

And now Kogan's earlier actions had an unexpected effect. British officers, whose shooting by the SS had been prevented when they were hidden in the camp, came up with a scheme to frighten the commandant into abandoning the evacuations. Using their plan, a British officer drafted a letter, supposedly from an officer of a British parachute regiment, addressed to the camp commandant, warning him not to undertake more transports of prisoners, on pain of retribution.

Kogan was in hiding along with the other forty-five wanted men. Once the plan to send the letter was approved, he came out of hiding to arrange, through the reliable squad leader Feld, to inform Dr. Ding-Schuler. Kogan arranged the details with Ding-Schuler, who was willing to send a police truck to Weimar, ostensibly to collect valuable instruments and vaccines. Kogan would be smuggled out inside a box in this truck, ending up at Ding-Schuler's house at Weimar. From there he could post the letter to commandant Pister. This was on April 8th. The truck's departure was delayed by an air raid, but after that the loading of the boxes, supervised by the invaluable Feld, and containing Kogan in one of them, proceeded without further trouble. Four hours later the letter was posted, bearing the all-important Weimar postmark.

Pister, already not in over-confident mood, hesitated still more when he received that letter. It bought time, but no-one knew just how much time they needed to hold out, how long before the Allied forces arrived. Their situation was so close to freedom and yet so perilous. Indeed, on April 7th those with senior block posts had been assembled and ordered to make preparations for the evacuation of the entire camp. They had decided this order should be ignored.

When the order to line up for roll call came no-one turned up. Called out to explain, the senior block inmates claimed that prisoners had refused the order because they were afraid of low-flying planes. Complete evacuation could not go ahead, though it was not possible to stop 6,000 being sent out that day. On the following day, April 8th, the SS appeared too disheartened to make another attempt to clear out the camp. Air-raid warnings continued, but provided only a temporary respite.

The camp committees decided to try to make contact with American troops who must be somewhere nearby. A transmitter, constructed some time before, had been considered too dangerous to use. Now, around noon on April 8th, using an agreed text for sending in Russian, German and English, the key personnel of the leadership of the resistance organisation gathered round the transmitter. The German-language transmission was being sent, when the electricity supply was suddenly cut off. Nothing daunted, the group got a generator operational. In a matter of minutes they could re-start sending. The Russian text of the SOS would be transmitted by Konstantin Ivanovitch Leonov. The Polish engineer expert Damazyn would transmit German and English versions.

The scene has been described by Teofil Witek, and recorded in the history of the camps' resistance by Hermann Langbein. The English text of their message goes like this: 'To the Allies. To the army of General Patton. This is Buchenwald concentration camp. SOS. We request help. They want to evacuate us. The SS wants to destroy us.'

The transmission was repeated, the set turned to receive. Only silence. Perhaps they bend forward to listen, perhaps they hear the faint extraneous sounds as they lean close to the set, straining hearing and imagination alike to believe at last a signal will end their isolation in this vigil of toil and struggle and playing for time. Imagine beads of sweat on the faces of the exhausted men, on the fingers of Damazyn as again, again, he sends the message. I see the pattern of whorls on his engrained fingertips. The very smell of their fear and their hope invades me – it is three minutes, an age-long three minutes, that they listen since the last transmission was made. At last. A message comes, holding their breath they bend their heads to listen for those faint sounds, their meaning, that emerges as: 'KZ.Bu. Hold out. Rushing to your aid. Staff of Third Army.'

Here I, recording this, merely state, that in a fever of excitement Damazyn fainted after this message came through. Indeed, I don't know what to comment. Except that, Damazyn fainted.

But it was not yet over. On April 9th, (though Dora was freed on that day) the resistance at Buchenwald had to watch helplessly as another 9,000 were marched away. The following day the commandant's staff packed their things. All camp documents were burned under the supervision of the SS, and another 9,280 men were forcefully cleared out from their blocks. They had sat there passively until the armed SS came with the call, 'Everyone out!' reinforced with kicks and blows.

Among those evicted were Czechs, the anti-Fascist core of the Polish military resistance, and the Soviet prisoners of war; by April 10th the 21,000 who remained in the camp had to watch while 28,285 marched away. One more day's delay would have seen their liberation. Then American planes circled overhead, their engines adding to the pandemonium howl of air raid warnings, the sirens sounding, the public-address system barking out, 'All SS men leave the camp immediately'. Artillery and rifle shots, the stutter of machine guns, grew louder. Commandant Pister called in the senior camp inmate, Hans Eiden, and a German called Edelmen. He transferred the command of the camp to them – while the SS evacuated themselves in a wild disorder of retreat. The hidden weapons would soon be taken out and distributed by the Austrian communist Franz Bera, in accordance with the instructions of the military leadership. Guards remained in the watchtowers and the barbed wire surround still had the electric current turned on. At around 3pm the watchtower guards began to surrender. A Wehrmacht soldier surrendered himself to a prisoner, telling him that American tanks were north of Weimar, moving onwards. Soon tanks and armoured cars were seen approaching over the Buchenwald mountain. At this the men of Buchenwald streamed out to meet them, stopping only to knock down the fences, and arresting any SS men they found.

Plan A, the plan for offensive action, was now being followed, the watchtowers and the main gate taken over by armed prisoners. One SS guard took off his white shirt and used it as a flag of surrender to armed men who were on the point of becoming ex-prisoners. Hans Eiden commandeered the public address system, announcing to the cheering crowd, 'Comrades, we are free!' An executive committee was chosen: a Russian, a Frenchman, a German, a Czech, an Italian, with Hans Eiden, elected as Head of Administration, receiving accreditation in that position by the American forces. Most of the first U.S. tanks hurriedly rolled on their way, as soldiers on the first two tanks casually told the prisoners, ordered on to Berlin. But on that first day of their freedom, there was sufficient ceremony. Eiden expressed everyone's thanks to the American army. An American officer is said to have replied, to enthusiastic cheering, that the army admired them for managing to preserve unity, order and strength despite the Nazi terror, adding, they were the best of Europe, and they had taken 150 SS men prisoner.

SACHSENHAUSEN

In 1938 German prisoners were assigned the task of building Sachsenhausen at a site near Berlin. (Its satellite Neuengamme, founded at around the same time, was classed as an independent camp in 1940. Two others, Stutthof, and Gross-Rosen, were set up in 1940.) Green and red-labelled men worked together at Sachsenhausen from the start. Equally oppressed, they formed sound working relationships. Jews arrived next, strictly segregated, not even allowed into the infirmary; earlier arrivals smuggled medicines into the Jewish blocks.

On the release of the senior inmate, Oskar Müller, in the spring of 1939, Harry Naujoks was nominated by the communist party group as a suitable replacement. Despite an initial reluctance, he did accept the job, holding it until transferred in 1942. On similar instructions Albert Buchman suppressed his doubts, to take on a position in the Labour Service. The power wielded by an armband-wearer was a terrible source of temptation, needing constant monitoring of what each person did; especially so as the communists were split into three groups, the pre-war prisoners, post-1935 prisoners espousing a popular-front policy, and those involved in disagreements on what followed from the Hitler-Stalin pact. Harmful political squabbles and conflicts of the Weimar period gradually healed as communists and social-democrats grew closer to each other. With more co-operation, general living conditions improved, lives were saved.

Non-political forms of opposition came from Jehovah's Witnesses, who had attracted the ire of the Nazi regime, by their refusal to give Nazi salutes or the greeting 'Heil Hitler'. Regarded as subversive elements, their publications, like their meetings, banned, sent from prisons to concentration camps, these purple-triangled men and women remained firm when war started, refusing the order to join up. For each one who said, 'No,' ten were shot. August Bickman was one who fearlessly went to execution. According to survivors, after he was dragged out and shot in the roll-call area, two men stepped forward from their line; asked if they were going to sign up, they replied, no, they had already signed but now they wished to withdraw their signatures. After more shootings, the SS gave up trying to get the Witnesses to fight. On Sundays about two hundred brethren huddled together in a barracks for Bible study; someone keeping watch. Even when their bibles were found, followed by the transfer of eighty Witnesses and the break-up of their integrated group by mixing them into other barracks, they were not disheartened, saying they had more opportunities for preaching to their fellow prisoners. (Named survivors from various camps feature in a video using film archive material, made by the Witnesses 'Watchtower' organisation.)

Jewish inmates continued to be subject to frightful treatment. It is much to the credit of the German communist Willi Marker that in spite of SS warnings not to go on with his efforts to ease their sufferings, he nonetheless persisted. He was sent to a penal unit, where a few nights later he was hanged. That was in April, 1940; his wife informed, with the words, 'Spouse committed suicide'.

Willi Marker was not alone in showing friendship to the Jews; one of the charges against Hermann Langbein for which he was locked in a punishment cell, was that he was on friendly terms with Jews and had tried to help them. And despite the extreme difficulties, Jewish prisoners took part in acts of resistance. The camp resistance had looked cautiously on plans made by the young Jewish group for open resistance. They had reason to dread the consequences of such actions. Perhaps a lesson had been learned, after Lambert Horn died. He had been a Reichstag delegate, he was a useful person in the infirmary. After his death on June 2nd 1939, he was laid out in the mortuary, flowers on his coffin. One by one the comrades came to pay him their last respects. The administration could not be kept in the dark; all the politicals who were hospital orderlies were brutally punished, and for some time after that political prisoners were barred from the hospital jobs, which was an unfortunate thing for the camp.

A group of the Czech students at first felt less than friendly towards their communist co-prisoners; yet by the time the group was released, before 1941, after enjoying spirited discussions which took place in the pathology department after dark, relations were such that a farewell party was thrown, where speeches, applause, and good feeling prevailed.

The proportion of those coming from occupied countries increased, non-Germans outnumbering Germans. The itch for political instruction still figured large. So when someone noticed a tattered-looking book among scrap items, he retrieved it – to the joy of the comrades, he'd found the Polish version of Stalin's book, 'Problems of Leninism'. A Marxist manual, in a Fascist camp! With care and reverence the text was cut up and distributed to Czech and Polish students for translation into German. Works by Lenin and Kautsky were smuggled in. A camp library, never discovered by the administration, had its beginnings with these unlikely volumes, used in political-education discussions. Books that found their way in included one from Karl Uhlrich on the Reichstag fire, given to a Polish prisoner with the information that the communists were organised, doing political work in the camp, that communistically-minded Czech students learned German and formed study groups based on the Marxist texts available. The Reichstag fire was a memorable event for the communists in camp, as it had been used by the Nazis, who may have organised its burning down – certainly it facilitated the passing of the 'Enabling Act', followed by as many repressive laws as were needed to eliminate the last vestiges of legal opposition to the State – as a pretext to arrest leading communists, Torgler and Dimitrov. Though Torgler was found not guilty, he was kept in 'protective custody' until his death; Georgi Dimitrov, who had promptly turned the tables on his accusers with a spirited speech during his trial, earned himself an acquittal, and his freedom.

Similar stuff got into a subsidiary camp, Berlin-Lichterfelde. Dissident workers in Berlin invited the Sachsenhausen comrades to study and comment on the draft policy programme put forward by the Saefkow group. Whether their suggestions on the final draft were incorporated or not, the Saefkow group sent them their warm greetings, expressing the wish that their links should be more than temporary, and would be beneficial to the party as a whole.

So important to them were these discussions, that a Russian, Nikolai Kyung, chosen to write a history of the revolution, (not the one in Russia, but the German revolution of 1918) was assigned to light working duties while he did so. The historical piece completed, it was translated into German, and used for study. More was needed to satisfy the comrades' hunger for secret political how-did-it-happen discussions; Janez Ranziger prepared lectures on the history of Yugoslavia, devoting particular attention to the question of how a relatively small population could resist the power of the German Reich. Conversations went on in one of the Jewish blocks, and in Czech and Polish groups too, with a young Pole, Tadeusz Patzer, allocated the task of producing a course on Marxism, culminating in a leaflet devoted to the tasks facing the national committee Free Germany,

The social-democrats were wary of these discussions, despite friendly co-operation with the organisers. Franz Bobzein took on leading positions, his attitudes and his courage attracting high praise from the Poles, who for the first time met a German person they could truly admire. Bobzein, Herbert Bender and Fritz Henssler, (two other social-democrats) formed a three-man committee organising cultural events; Bender's 'literary evenings' included scenes from 'Faust', while Dutchmen celebrated Christmas 1943 by singing a song of historical struggle against occupying forces. The evening events, at first put on secretly, later acquired a semi-legal status, with entry by ticket for the fortunate few who, after the day's toil, the litre of thin soup, found mental escape to the land of lost content, or in the case of 'Faust', discontent.

It took a Viennese Jew, Fritz Hirsch, to introduce ideology into the concerts which the SS allowed, and attended. He daringly entertained with his own songs, songs with lines like, 'You can make a zebra lame, but the zebra won't get tame.' Such an obvious reference to the striped uniforms of the camp could hardly have been misunderstood by the SS, but Hirsch got away with it. Poems were written – a notebook, found buried in the foundations, contained forty poems written by a Russian prisoner. Russian and Ukrainian prisoners had arrived in September 1942, very different in their politics and their languages; Russians prisoners-of-war, Ukrainians mostly in Germany as workers. The Russians tended to operate as a group, daring and determined in their escape attempts. In work situations they could be relied on - set to work constructing a munitions factory, a Russian contingent completed their task so successfully that sections of walling collapsed, nor was the plant ever operational.

Information on daily events features in a diary kept by Emil Buge, an interpreter for the dreaded political department, thereby enabled to work late in the office, recording details, his diary smuggled out when reliable men were due for release, on occasions such as Hitler's birthday. Buge pasted his noted-down information in spectacle cases released men could take out with them. Learning of his own impending release, he prepared more spectacle cases for his successor Heinrich Lienau to use. From these notes we know of a revolt planned by Ukrainians in 1942. They had a number of sharpened pocket knives and daggers, but were caught. Their ringleaders confessed. The Ukrainians were equally unlucky with their buried radio, found in the forest where an outside detail worked.

Two relief schemes for those most in need of extra food depended on the secret organisation's argument that those who had access to more food through Red Cross parcels, should share with others. The daily bread ration was called Kuhle, so the German communists referred to their re-distribution scheme as 'Rote Kuhle', Red Bread. The camp administration turned a blind eye to it, though when the scheme was betrayed to the Gestapo, reprisals followed – the Gestapo would dearly have liked to discover the members of the secret organisation they suspected but were unable to track down.

The administration actually approved of a second relief scheme, whereby Norwegian prisoners, a privileged group, regularly gave their surplus Red Cross food to Russian prisoners of war. The senior camp inmate at the time was Heinz Bartsch, another of the German communists who used their posts to help others. So the decision was, that each recipient of a food parcel gave his bread ration for the day to another person. Bartsch was exposed through this, and lost his life, shot for this 'communist relief action'; but his life is such a demonstration of a practical love for one's fellow men that, remembered by those who knew him with reverence, the tale of his unswerving humanity reverberates as hope for mankind.

Communist groups in Berlin still functioned in 1944; with contacts established, plotting prisoners were assigned to outside work in Berlin. Thus they met civilians, some of whom helped several prisoners to escape and continue their work in the illegal Berlin organisation, while in the Heinkel works, the politicals in the outside details made contact early that year with about one hundred of the civilian workers. The dedicated prisoners gave these workers regular political instruction.

This Heinkel aircraft factory was a huge enterprise, with 5,000 prisoners of various nationalities at work there, a number of whom used quantities of the Plexiglas intended for the aircrafts' windows to make cigarette lighters. Civilian workers bought or bartered for these. A speciality of a group of young Russians was the removal of small valves, replacements for which took a long time to arrive; damaging machinery and equipment were occupations willingly undertaken by the slave labourers as their particular contribution to the war effort. Sometimes a worker would smuggle out letters for them. But on 27th March the camp administration caught someone listening to a radio. Worse, the search that followed revealed leaflets proposing illegal actions in the Ruhr. These instructions of the resistance committee to those working in the war factories were, to do the work slowly, produce substandard articles, waste materials, damage machinery. After all this advice was found by the SS, investigations, arrests, transfers to other camps with executions of communists, followed swiftly after.

In touch with civilian workers, prisoners were at this stage of the war able to meet well-disposed people. At the subsidiary camp of Glau, construction site supervisors and even SS technicians behaved decently. One of the escapers, Rudolf Wunderlich, commented most favourably on an ordinary non-political Berliner, a woman who worked as a cleaner in the Main Security Office. This Annie Noack risked her safety to help prisoners, she even walked off with an official stamp from the Office for the prisoners to use in preparing false papers. Another cleaning woman, a boiler room attendant, other craftsmen, also helped; ordinary people, showing extraordinary courage.

Gestapo suspicions of a communist conspiracy resulted in a special commission investigating relief actions; that was when Heinz Bartsch and his fellow helpers were arrested and shot. The commission investigated in July 1944, by which time the camp was so large as to be difficult, from the German viewpoint, to manage with any degree of efficiency. The administration relied on information from numerous informers, but also felt endangered by the Gestapo's probings. The Gestapo had learned that the camp's SS men had the habit of using criminal prisoners to steal and pass on to them the hidden valuables of murdered men. In the interests of a cover-up, the administration was not averse to anyone hindering the investigating commission; so political prisoners did their bit for their own reasons, providing the two hundred or so very dangerous informers with false information. Additionally, office reports and roll calls needed for the smooth running of the camp did not work efficiently. The report-writer responsible for such records having both competence and much experience, he was suspected, correctly, of obstructive tactics. But given the administration's pre-occupation with bureaucracy, he could not be immediately dismissed from his job. The commission, unable to prove communists were undermining their chief informer, proposed that report-writer Harter, their suspect, should be released from protective custody in order to train a successor, so he could then be replaced as report writer.

The red-triangles had worked their way into holding most of the office jobs. They kept the camp running, but with attitudes and actions helpful to the prisoners' community. They were, for instance, able to read informers' reports. But the brutality of the commission created a critical situation for the resistance organisation. The worst damage resulted from betrayal by the senior camp inmate, Kuhnke. His work for the SS and Gestapo resulted, amongst other tragic events, in thirty men shot, and another 103 put on a transport to Mauthausen. But they had managed to get Kuhnke included in the same transport as the 103. He was made to march at their head, reportedly trembling and crying, begging for his life, reviled by those who knew him as a heartless murderer.

Escapes – three in 1942 – became more feasible. It was easier to get away from sub-camps, easier too to get help from outside. Although in 1943 nobody got away, in 1944 ninety-six made it, and in the early part of 1945, 288. An unusual escape by tunnel was achieved by British Air Force officers, sent to Sachsenhausen after their failed escape attempt from a POW camp. By 1945, with the end for Hitler drawing near, more Sachsenhausen lives were put on the line. Nineteen Luxembourgers had refused to join the SS. Together with Russian and British prisoners of war, they were condemned to death, tied up and led out of the camp in the dead of night. The Luxembourger Victor Reuland seized a gun from one of the guards and shot him. Back in the camp, friends heard the rattle of machine guns; and knew how the guards had responded.

Max Opitz had made a skeleton key to an SS weapons store. With the camp police under the command of a feared green kapo, and after the mass executions and general terror caused by the special commission, it would take some ingenuity, not to mention nerve, to use it to add to the few weapons already acquired from SS offices in Berlin. The situation was even more dire after transports to Mauthausen and the recruitment of prisoners, only in name voluntary, into a specially formed army unit called the Dirlewanger Unit.

In the middle of March 1945, with the Soviet armies approaching, Danes and Norwegians were protected by the Swedish Red Cross. There were still 40,000 prisoners held; the weakened resistance movement could not stop the next stage of the Nazi plan. All that could be done was for trustworthy comrades with military experience to act as auxiliary guards on the evacuation marches north, their task in bringing up the rear. to keep the SS from killing those who fell behind. To guard those remaining in the camp, a prepared group known as the 'hose guard' (it had camouflaged its preparations for taking on the role of a military unit by regular fire-fighting practice) would be allocated responsibility.

5,000 people remained. These included women, and patients in the hospital, unfit to be moved out. The protective group of 'hose guards' had the task of preventing the hospital from being blown up, the patients killed. And defying SS orders, some four hundred healthy volunteers, about two hundred of them women, about forty Reds, had decided to stay, to care for the weak and ill.

On April 20th the evacuation began. It was evening. Groups of five hundred women, then five hundred men, five hundred more, more, from that evening on throughout the night and all the next day until 11 p.m. After that the gate stayed shut, the block leaders told to leave. Instead of SS men, the 'hose guard' occupied the watchtowers. The machine gun from Tower A was moved onto the camp road. Food supplies and storage areas were put under guard. SS men were found hiding, disarmed and driven out of the camp. It became very quiet. All precautions had been taken against the return of SS forces.

Sunday morning, the 22nd – a Sunday with no roll call, no guards except their own guard at the gate. Waiting. The tense and eerie silence. At 11 o'clock shouts of, 'Ruskie, Ruskie, the Russians are here!' A rush to the roll call area, there were the Red Army men, soon being hugged, kissed – and then the troops must hurriedly move on. So freedom came at Sachsenhausen. Later it was learned that the committee's tactic of sending trusted men as guards for the column of evacuees had some good results. A ex-Reichstag deputy of the social-democratic party, Fritz Henssler, who was sixty, dropped by the side of the road exhausted, expecting to be finished off by a pistol shot to the neck. On a baggage cart at the end of the line Karl Sauer, a veteran of the Spanish civil war, recognised Henssler, sitting in a ditch. Sauer and his comrades insisted he must be rescued and ride on a wagon. Despite objections from the SS, this was done, and without SS retaliation.

NEUENGAMME

1938, another satellite of Sachsenhausen, Neuengamme: in 1940 classed as an independent camp. German criminals were in charge of day-to-day arrangements, but soon political prisoners began to change the atmosphere. 870 politicals were among the 2,800 Germans imprisoned there. Albin Lüdke from the Work Assignments was one who did outstanding work at an automatic rifle-making factory, where go-slows and sabotage were the recommended forms of resistance.

Fritz Bringmann, a survivor, wrote about his camp experience as a nurse. Ordered to inject weak and ill Russian prisoners-of-war with carbolic acid, he refused to obey. Other nursing staff followed his lead. Though they were beaten, their punishment stopped at that. Compassionate SS doctors were thin on the ground, not to say highly unusual. When Dr. Benno Adolph arrived at Neuengamme, he asked an unprecedented question, 'Where can I help?' After the war, when this doctor was arrested by the Russians, he was released after prisoners testified on his behalf. Similarly, when he was arrested by the Americans, Poles and Russians secured his release by again speaking up for him.

Quirky behaviour can stick in the mind. It was recalled by Hans Christian Meier that a kapo, notorious for his brutality, nevertheless refused to punish those due for a beating in the roll call area. He said he'd never beaten anyone on orders in his life, and he never would. He himself was beaten and sent to the punishment cells.

The end drew near. When those of German nationality at the main camp were conscripted into the so-called Dirlewanger unit, some made their escape in the general confusion on May 2nd, joining with resistance groups in Hamburg, while others in the depleted resistance groups discussed the feasibility of a rebellion. With three pistols! The Belgian André Mandryckxs was one of the noted activists of the camp's international resistance committee, which met on February 25th in groups of three and five, to discuss what they could do. Before any decision was made, the evacuation of prisoners began, continuing every day for a week. This led to a major tragedy the resistance proved powerless to prevent – but at least they tried.

The commandant's dilemma was, where could he send the prisoners on to. He sent them to Lübeck. There, along with thousands of others from various subsidiary camps, they were put aboard ships, so that about 11,000 were held in Lübeck Bay. All the ships were being heavily bombed by Allied planes.

The prisoners formed an action committee. They tried to contact a certain captain. Seven Russians volunteered to swim to the shore to tell the Allies they were on board ship so the Allied air-raids on them would be called off. No swimmer reached the shore. The ships' captains were ordered to put out to sea, knowing that all ships were being bombed and sunk. The captain of the smallest ship refused the order, but the two large ships sailed out to the open sea. On May 3rd they were sunk. Only a few prisoners lived to tell the tale, one of them a Jehovah's Witness.

On 5th May British troops reached Neuengamme Camp. It was too late. They found it empty.

A small subsidiary camp, Hallein, has a story of its ending, unique, and inspiring. The Austrians who worked in a quarry had long been in contact with communists in the nearby town of Hallein. They knew American forces were drawing near. By May

5th, the war teetering to its close, the SS left Hallein, but the prisoners were still under guard, and the camp had no food supply. One of the resistors wrote a secret note to their contact Agnes Primocic in Hallein town. This comrade sprang into action; she put on a Red Cross uniform, and rode on her bike to the quarry. Storming into the camp office, she threatened the officer-in-charge with retribution from the Americans, if anything should happen to the prisoners. The man who had sent her the note was brought in, and involved in the discussions. A decision was reached; the officer-in-charge would escort the prisoners into the town – provided that the mayor had no objections – and at 11pm they marched off together, all forty-seven of them plus their guards, to food and shelter in the town of Hallein.

FLOSSENBÜRG

'Greens' were put in possession of armband posts at Flossenbürg, set up in 1938 ready for non-German prisoners expected when war began. But when in November 1942 eight 'Reds', including Naujoks, were transferred from Sachsenhausen, the SS intending to keep them in strict isolation before finishing them off, they were thwarted by Green armband-wearers who had ideas of their own. The senior inmate, (described by Franz Ahrens as 'a gentleman thief') took the view that as these newcomers had treated them as comrades when they themselves had been in Sachsenhausen, they might be sure they too would be helped. They lived on.

Acts of sabotage at Flossenbürg included the burying of steel plates intended for tanks. French engineers and technicians working in an aircraft plant near the satellite camp at Floha devised a system for making defective rivets, and expertly produced parts bound to fail with heavy use.

A rebellion of Russian prisoners of war in the satellite camp Mulsen-St. Micheln has been described by the chronicler of Flossenbürg, Toni Siegert. The prisoners contrived to exchange messages with some of their comrades doing forced labour in Leipzig. Their meagre food rations had been cut several times. On the night of May 1st – 2nd 1944 they took action. The fuses for the buildings' lighting system were removed. Mattresses were set on fire, home-made knives used against oppressive prisoner-functionaries. But the guards were too strong and well-armed for the break-out to succeed. The ringleaders, if not stabbed or shot at the time of the uprising, were transferred to the main camp and there executed.

When the camp neared its end, as Siegert recalled, the most they could do in the final evacuation was to help people escape, and provide food and cigarettes. About 1,500 patients and others who went into hiding to avoid being marched away are believed to have put up resistance to the SS, before being liberated by US troops on April 23rd.

RAVENSBRÜCK

Ravensbrück, the notorious camp set up for women near Berlin, started off on 5th May 1939, gathering together women from vastly different backgrounds. 867 women had been sent from another camp to build it. Many of these were still-surviving Jehovah's Witnesses. Of 2,000 early inmates, a large contingent were German women tagged with the black triangle of the 'anti-socials'; by 1942 the count had swelled to 10,800, with many 'politicals' added to the mix. German women arrested for political reasons formed a reliable group, protecting women from medical experiments and sterilisations.

Czech, French, Dutch, and Polish contingents included 'politicals' like Mila Milotova – caught in Czechoslovakia helping fugitives to hide and in running an illegal press – or Norwegian Meta Christiansun who made illegal identity cards for underground workers. Such people, assets to the resistance. Polish women also, who found ways to get information and messages out from the sub-camps. At least one worker from the Siemen's plant helped the prisoners; he was caught, he and his family sent to a camp.

A feature of Ravensbrück was its use by the administration as a training ground for women who volunteered for the SS. As many as 3,500 went through that training. 150 were appointed as guards; the pay for such work was higher than for their previous civilian work.

As in all the camps, it was vital for resistors to save lives, undertake sabotage, maintain their mental life, organise educational work. Wanda Kiedrzynska, a Polish woman, included escape as one of the aims of her group. Russians and Czechs figure among the names of those deleted from lists of women intended to be killed for their resistance activities. A discussion group subject, 'What is a nation?' indicates a problem that pre-occupied Austrian prisoners in more than one camp. Austrians in Ravensbrück maintained good contacts with the Czechs and the French women, but avoided Germans communists. Political and cultural hatchets needed to be buried; the November 1942 celebration included in its programme both a talk about the Russian revolution and songs and recitations.

The Girl Scouts' group, named in Ravensbrück as 'Mury', saw their main purpose quite clearly: to develop altruistic behaviour. The members of this group, started in 1941, wanted to live, and to help others live too. They were neither nationalistic nor anti-Semitic. When large numbers of children were sent to Ravensbrück after the crushed Warsaw rising, these Polish scouts, trained by the Scoutmistress Jozefa Kontor, who had prepared her scouts for their secret role through a teacher-training programme, started an educational experience unique in the camps.

Educational activities also appealed to Olga Benario. She had been an officer of the German Communist Party, and now as senior block inmate she set herself the task of organising a broad-based cultural programme of courses and literary evenings where the poetry of Goethe, Schiller and others was recited; books and plays the prisoners had read in their old free lives were discussed, poems recited, written, too, all part of the process of keeping active minds. Dutch women wrote a pamphlet with no politics in it except for the politics of cheering their fellow-women up. And on Christmas Day 1944, astonishingly, these women persuaded the administration to allow a celebration for the children of the camp, a few festive moments on that day to brighten the children's lives.

Austrian women remember an occasion when three Austrian Jews, transferred by their comrades in Auschwitz to avoid execution, were in need of protection. Danuta, a Polish senior block inmate, a formidable woman who headed the secret organisation, was applied to for help. Another prisoner objected on the grounds of political differences with the newly-arrived women. Though Danuta held strong Polish nationalist opinions, she immediately pointed out that these were sister inmates, everything else was of secondary importance. So it was too for Else Krug, held in the penal block. Sent to the camp as an 'anti-social', the term used for classifying prostitutes, she was ordered to whip a woman for some misdemeanour. Else refused to do it. In spite of being assured that if she did use the whip she'd be let out of the penal block and be rewarded with more food, she still would not. For her refusal she was put on a transport of women going to be gassed.

As the war situation became dire for the German army, so the importance to them of meeting production targets in the factories increased. Fifty-four Russian women, keenly aware of this, refused work in arms factories and despite punishments, kept up their refusal until threatened with being shot; they then changed tactics, embarking on systematic sabotage. Poles as well as Russians, very determined and courageous, lost many brave people, sentenced to death for sabotage. About 600 Jehovah's Witnesses who did sewing work staunchly refused to sew up bags for Army use. Though kept standing in the cold for five days they held firm. Ninety among them refused work in the gardening details or the Angora wool-breeding section, because the vegetables were destined for an SS field hospital, the rabbits' wool for military purposes. One refused to appear for roll call. Nor would they unload straw for Army horses, sticking to their refusals in spite of being whipped, subjected to extreme cold and all but starved; transferred to Auschwitz, mere walking skeletons, they were defiant still.

Workers in the prison hospital were life-savers. Endangered prisoners had their numbers exchanged with the help of Work Assignment and Clothing Depot clerks, for those of dead prisoners. Information from prisoners about the intended gassing of 700 women, sent out and broadcast on Allied radios, put a stop to it. When the SS intended to kill women who'd suffered medical experimentation they were able to point out to the SS that the details of what they'd done and when they'd done it were already known to the world. This gave the SS reason to pause, and gained the resistance time to arrange help for the women. Thanks to this, women mutilated by medical experiments were hidden, then transported away to a factory. Three more endangered Austrian Jewish women were spotted on arrival, removed from the transport they had come on, hidden to evade the SS search, renumbered by Nadja Persic, a Yugoslav doctor who gave them French women's identities. They were then sent off with an International Red Cross group alerted by the Norwegian Silvia Salverson's detailed report, to Sweden, in April 1945, as the camp neared its end.

Preparations for protecting 26,700 women in the main camp and girls in detention camps for minors went ahead. In the rush of events it sadly proved impossible to stop the evacuation on April 25th. All except hospital patients, some medical staff, and several women who stayed behind to help care for the weak and ill, had to go. Five days of transition followed the SS departure. Then, on the camp road, appeared the first Soviet soldiers. The next day detachments of their troops arrived at the camp; it was liberated, on the famous day of May 1st.

BERGEN-BELSEN

Bergen-Belsen: the only camp handed over, on Himmler's order, to Allied forces at the war's end. Perhaps this accounts for photographic evidence a-plenty recording the state of the survivors, and why the name 'Belsen' is sometimes used as if synonymous with the term 'concentration camp'.

It had started as something like a transit camp, in that Jews sent there were considered suitable for an exchange with German nationals interned abroad. When in 1943 the camp was transferred to the control of the Economic Office it also housed Jewish political prisoners segregated into separate barracks – until work requirements made such isolation impracticable. There were children there too. In Hannah Levy-Hauss' diary she wrote in August 1944 of her efforts to provide education for 110 children in her block. Their ages ranged from three to fifteen. The task was immensely difficult. But a theatrical performance for them took place, staged by Dutch Jews. That was on August 31st, the Dutch queen's birthday; the Dutch women were celebrating it as a political statement, just as the French had celebrated their national day, in their washroom, on the 14th of July.

An entry in Hannah's diary on October 17th 1944, tells of a rebellion by Polish women, whether politicals or Jewish she did not know. Alarmed, the SS ordered everyone to return to barracks. In the kitchens the fires were put out. Gates sectioning off different parts of the camp were locked. Though nothing more of the prisoners' revolt was known for Hannah to record, its suppression became evident when she saw the camp crematorium. It was operating non-stop. Even Hermann Langbein can only comment that no other sources tell more of this, wondering; how many other undocumented camp revolts were there?

In the early months of 1945, when evacuation marches from other camps brought more and more contingents of exhausted prisoners to Bergen-Belsen, conditions there became unbearable. The situation was quite different from camps where a disciplined underground organisation could see to distributing food fairly, organising such work within the camp as was needed to keep up necessary functions in a place where many people lived. The French doctor G. L. Frejefon helped, by the kindness and understanding he showed his disease-ridden patients. By April 1st another diarist, Abel Herzberg, recorded that no roll calls were held, no work done. People just died. Without the strengthening thread of a uniting consciousness to animate them, how could they retain the inner fortitude needed for them to keep alive? The few who did survive recall no such hopeful ethos in those critical days.

On the 6th, the evacuations started. It was not until the 15th that, by the agreement negotiated with Himmler, British troops entered the camp. The state of it then is more widely known about than the stories of its resistors. It is enough to say that dysentery was rife, water supplies not distributed, food the SS had in plenty remained in store. Had there been an unbroken resistance group to bring the unifying framework of an agreed plan, those last days might have been less horrible. That there was not, was not the fault of the imprisoned; it was the fault of those who put them there, those who would not believe these were death camps and those who knew and said nothing. The photographic evidence convinced, at last, an unbelieving world.

Nor did the liberation on that beautiful spring morning, with its aftermath for survivors moved to nearby army barracks, take place without further heartbreak. Many had no wish to return to countries where people clearly did not want them. Survivors wanted their Jewishness to be acknowledged in preference to their nationality, as a rebuttal of the 'final solution' and an assertion of their right to choose. As they gradually regained strength – even though they resented the unpalatable diet Allied doctors supplied them in well-meaning efforts to find out what starved people could best be fed with, thousands did to some extent recover. Their resentment grew at being called 'DP's, displaced persons, living in barracks behind a wire surround. During the five or six years of their stay, the equivalent of resistance arose in the form of a thriving cultural life. Concerts were organised, newspapers produced, schools set up, with the aim of giving purpose and meaning back to emptied lives in limbo there; plays that rehearsed their camp situation helped to purge, cabarets and jokey performances gave the relief of laughter. Musical talent re-surfaced, and concerts there and at other camps emphasised an undiminished humanity.

For those Jews encountering hostility in countries they went back to, and who therefore decided they would make their way to Palestine, the 'DP' camp became a staging post on their way to a still-illegal journey; stealing and smuggling skills were put to use to smuggle arms intended for the fight against British troops when they got to Palestine.

MAJDANEK

Majdanek was a late-opening camp, built to take Russian prisoners of war; many did not intend staying there if courage could free them. In March 1942 several dozen escaped. Only one was recaptured. That summer, about eighty to a hundred more escaped by arranging their blankets in piles of five and heaping them onto the barbed wire. They simply climbed over and dispersed into the fields. Four of them were shot, but the others got away – they had chosen a suitably dark night.

The camp came under Central Administration in November 1943, bringing other nationalities to join the Russians. The Polish contingent played a large part in morale-raising activities such as those thought up by paedriatician Miecyslaw Michalowicz, who presented medical lectures when work was at last over for the day.

Escapes continued. In the summer of 1944 a German kapo and nine Polish prisoners took to their heels, meeting up with others in a partisan unit. Nineteen Russians and a German kapo were transferred to the special detail at Auschwitz. Their strength and spirit assisted resistance work there. Then the Soviet armies drew near. Majdanek was evacuated and closed down.

MAUTHAUSEN

Mauthausen camp, with its subsidiary at Gusen, was the first camp set up in Austria – after the 'Anschluss' in 1938. Melk and Loiblpass camps were nearby, providing cheap labour for arms factories and quarries. 1939 saw four escapes, two of them successful; by the end of 1940 seven more attempts.

'Red triangle' wearers – first Czechs, then, in May 1940, Poles, and not long after that Spaniards, (including veterans of the Spanish civil war) swelled the numbers, but the Spaniards suffered enormous loss of life, with 4,200 out of 7,500 dead by the end of 1942. A group of Rumanian Jews, (in October 1940, before the politically-minded prisoners gained positions from the original 'green' armband wearers) all veterans of the anti-Fascist fight in Spain, were being systematically murdered. Determined that if they could not live, at least they would die with dignity, six of them walked towards a watchtower. They sang as they walked, they advanced singing, not songs of mourning, they sang the 'International'. The guards called 'Halt!' But they walked on, the sound of their singing heard by their fellow-prisoners, heard against the rattle of machine-gun fire.

The Spanish contingent, organised as far back as their internment in France following Franco's victory, kept their cohesion, forming a tight group that worked to improve the appalling conditions. Shared language knowledge helped them make contact with International Brigaders from the Spanish war, who had likewise been interned in France before Mauthausen. The awful death rates showed the urgent need for a camp resistance organisation which could overcome the prisoners' differences in politics, nationality and religion, which it suited the SS to exploit. After much discussion to sort out mutual distrusts, international links between Spaniards, Germans, Austrians, Czechs, French, Rumanians, Russians, Italians and Hungarians were brought about. Among the practical successes following from this, Istvan Balogh, a Hungarian veteran of the Spanish civil war, had help from his old comrades in building a radio with parts he stole from his place of work. This was in September 1941. He listened to news broadcasts, careful only to pass on that information to a select band of brothers. Other radios, cherished items, included one hidden in the crematorium and a crystal set that Dr. Vratislav Busek could sometimes listen to in the hospital.

Eight prisoners escaped in 1941, two getting clean away. In 1942 three out of eleven succeeded; they were from a subsidiary camp at Vocklabruck, where a maid helped them. With wire-cutters they'd asked her for, the prisoners cut through the fences and made for the mountains.

By chance, a general disinfection of the camp was scheduled the same day Germany attacked the Soviet Union. Outside the huts the prisoners, already stripped off, heard the loudspeakers blaring out announcements of the German invasion. The noise of these provided the Spaniards with cover for a swift exchange of information and views for setting up secret groups, placing people in useful places such as the office, with as wide a representation of national groups as possible.

Intrigues for positions of influence continued. The chief camp clerk, described by the survivor Hans Marsalek as a Viennese con-man more brutal in his attitude than the SS, nicknamed the King of Mauthausen, strutted about the camp wearing white gloves, making not inconsiderable use of morphine from the hospital supplies. The strategy adopted by the camp plotters to rid themselves of this tyrant was to increase his morphine supply until his behaviour became so eccentric that the commandant deposed him and transferred him to Gusen. There prisoners who knew him gave him a hard time. Eventually, dangerous to the SS because of his knowledge of their crimes, he was 'shot while trying to escape'. Mauthausen prisoners heaved sighs of relief when a Czech, an Austrian and a Spaniard took over. But Mauthausen, and Gusen too, remained in the overall charge of green senior camp inmates until the end. This meant, among other things, that food parcels, which were of immense importance in the struggle to survive, were unlikely to reach those they were intended for.

The Russian Major Ivan Alexayevich Panfilov gained a useful position in the laundry-drying detail; in Gusen and another sub-camp at the Steyr Works, seasoned comrades were beavering away to disrupt the system despite all difficulties. When large numbers of Austrians arrived, (classed by the German authorities as German) these Austrians were placed where they might get information out to fellow-Austrians and, using their initiative, organise solidarity actions. One who came to the fore was Josef Kohl. Leo Gabler, too, who arrived at the camp in 1943, played an active part, while the Czech Marsalek became known for his great courage.

By 1943, twenty-five out of forty-four made successful escapes. In 1944, out of 126 attempts, twenty-eight successes. Kaspar Bachl, a German, in the subsidiary camp Klagenfurt, maintained some contact with his wife. With her help, on November the 15th 1944 he got away, to be hidden by anti-Nazis at Fuschl until the war was over.

In-camp discussions on the national problem of whether Austria should remain annexed by Germany after the war, together with Marxist political discussions, went ahead, no doubt heatedly, with very varying viewpoints expressed – the ability to think and argue evidently not extinguished. Survivors acquired a better understanding of each other's position than had existed pre-war. The Polish contingent clung most closely to nationalistic ideas; they alone had no representatives on the international resistance committee.

Changing conditions made it more difficult for the administration to prevent escapes or bring back hunted-down men for punishment. Escape attempts rose in 1945 to 339, 310 successful. On February 1st 1945 Josef Lauscher made a daring flit from an outside working detail in Vienna, prepared for him by the Mauthausen resistance group after Lauscher was transferred from Dachau as punishment for his activities. On the group's initiative, he was supplied with clothes, money, a razor blade, and addresses of safe houses in Vienna. Transferring him to the satellite camp in Vienna meant circumventing an SS ruling that no prisoner could be transferred to an outside detail in a camp in his own home town. Marsalek, the chief mover in the plan, altered the office's file entry. Lauscher's home town, 'Wien', changed to 'Wiener-Neustadt'. At a crucial moment of this escape a building superintendent let Lauscher take cover in her apartment, and did not betray him. He was able to make his way to a safe house.

Cyrankiewicz arrived on the Mauthausen scene in 1945, together with other Poles transferred from Auschwitz. His knowledge of the complex of attitudes among Poles from many different backgrounds enabled useful understandings to develop in other-nationality prisoners. Poles made great efforts to maintain their cultural life, including recitations of poems about their people's rebirth after oppression. Seven Poles are known to have written poems, or composed music. A Professor Omicki not only gave geography lectures, he treated those in his block to commentaries on the world situation. By the summer of 1943 Czechs and Spaniards evolved a relatively open cultural life within their ethnic groups, while a French radio technician, Serge Choumoff had the name, 'radio chronicler' bestowed on him for his activities at Gusen.

A Russian-led resistance group had shaky beginnings, but did develop plans for armed uprising. Valentin Sakharov and Franz Dahlem were its leading lights. A Spaniard joined in organisational tasks, opposing the effects of national, political and religious differences; Spaniards, including socialists, anarchists and republicans, took the lead in overcoming prejudice against the large contingent of French who arrived in 1943, by explaining they were anti-Fascists like themselves, rather than the collaborationists they were assumed to be.

Sakharov has given us an appreciative account of a doctor, Josef Podloha, who had been a professor at the University of Brno. One anecdote tells how after treating a member of an SS man's family, he was asked what he wanted as a reward. He replied that he wanted, not cigarettes or food, but for the prisoners to be less cruelly beaten. In May 1942, appointed physician-in-chief at the hospital, he, and doctors working to his directions, saved many lives. Towards the end, with his colleague Vratislav Brusek, he persuaded the camp commandant to reduce the numbers of those marked down to be gassed. And of the French doctors, Paul Tillard reports that Dr Quennouille was so outstanding that hundreds owed their lives to him. Those not 'in the know' mostly never learned how some apparently miraculous last-minute reprieve came about, or who they owed their lives to.

Through the international resistance a Czech, Kunes Pany, obtained the post of chief clerk. Among his outstanding achievements, he managed to smuggle in arms. Even those usually critical of communists have spoken of Pany as a man above reproach, immeasurably helpful.

Clergymen sometimes seized opportunities to send information out. Johannes Gruber's camp job was as kapo to a detail conserving prehistoric artefacts from excavations. Via his sister in Linz-Uhrfahr, he conserved information about the camp too, sending it on to France, Czechoslovakia and Poland. Gruber was not a professional conspirator; too-frequent exchanges of letters and packages came to the attention of the SS. Notes and documents found in his possession could not be explained away. He was first beaten, then shot, his outside contacts arrested and tortured – and the central administration forbade the use of clergymen for any secretarial duties.

The SS were right to fear the secret activities of those who carried out secretarial tasks for them. Franscisco Baux, working in the police records department, secretly copied photographs of important visitors to the camp, and some of its victims. His Spanish organisation hid this evidence for two years, until the time of liberation. And in December 1944, a squad of twenty men sent to the euthanasia department at Hartheim Castle with orders to destroy all evidence of the use of poison gas, rightly suspected that they too were regarded as evidence to be destroyed when their task was done; a Spaniard among them wrote the information on a slip of paper and put it in a bottle. Hidden in a wall near the door to the gas chamber, his testimony was found after the war.

Work assignment records at Mauthausen were saved by Sibile Jose Bailina, another of the Spanish contingent. And Czechs working in the office saved the death records from January 7th 1939 to April 29th 1945. Work Assignment clerks, taking enormous risks, kept a considerable number of prisoners from being assigned to any work details, by falsifying the numbers of prisoners. Some – for instance the Polish aristocrat Badeni – could never have survived hard labour, and though saved by those who seemed to him to be having an easy time of it, would have no idea of what was secretly undertaken on his behalf.

The resistance movement transferred a number of reliable Frenchmen to the satellite camp of Melk. One of these, his real name André Ulmann, was known as Antonin Pichon, concealing from the SS that he was a Jew and enabling him to serve as camp clerk. He it was who maintained contact with the secret group in the main camp, playing a decisive part in the Melk group, which included different nationalities and shades of opinion. An example of the good relationships between groups, is the agreement, similar to mutual help elsewhere, reached between communists and catholics; when Catholics held a Mass, a communist kept watch, and when communists held a meeting, then a Catholic obliged by watching out for the guards until the meeting was over. Ulmann also worked with the resistance group to influence the guards, some of whom were Austrian.

Hungarian Jews from the communist section had smuggled in several loaded revolvers when they were transferred, and took these weapons with them when the next move came, to Ebensee. Also evacuated to Ebensee as the Russian army approached, the French group strengthened the resistance they found established there, a French group which called itself 'National Front', embracing communists, Gaullists, socialists and non-political members, with links to the other national groups. The international group set itself to delay the building of a factory intended to be constructed in a tunnel, out of the way of Allied bombing raids, the delay effective enough for the factory never to come into operation – the Russians were coming.

At the quarry near Melk, on forced labour, the attitude of both the manager, an old Austrian monarchist, and the guard, an Austrian anti-Fascist conscripted into the SS eased prisoners' sufferings. The manager and his wife were arrested – after the regulation torture for giving prisoners food, the wife's foot had to be amputated. Nor were that couple the only humane persons in charge. A sub-camp at Wiener Neustadt had a master, known only as Gunter, who brought prisoners food and dressed wounds from beatings. At yet another sub-camp, Loiblpass, the known proximity of partisans encouraged escape attempts. In 1944 a Pole working on an outside detail killed his guard and reached the mountains, but only stayed free for six days before recapture and death. A few days later three Russian officers knocked down three guards, took their clothes and weapons and tied them up. Driving in their vehicle to the other side of the pass, unchallenged, in SS uniforms, they headed off for the partisans. Three Frenchmen from the same detail got away, helped by a civilian Croatian worker. Concealed in the false bottom of a dumper truck they, too, reached the partisans. Later that year, four Frenchmen working outside the camp laying telephone lines overcame their guards. Reaching the mountains, they too joined a partisan group.

Mauthausen's overcrowded conditions in its later days, 1944 to 1945, together with the alarmed state of the camp administration, had as its up-side opportunities to save lives. The armband-wearers staffing the office and hospital made false reports and re-numbered prisoners. After a warning from the office staff, an Austrian communist, Leopold Kuhn, had an identity-swap, with Kuhn admitted to hospital until a suitable substitute was found, a man called Robert Litterer who died from typhus after transfer from Gross-Rosen. Kuhn was reported dead in his place, and transferred to a camp where he would not be recognised by officialdom. Indeed, after liberation Kuhn reported he had considerable difficulty in proving his true identity, for his discharge papers were in the name of Litterer.

News from the outside world obtained from secret radios, though vital, was extremely dangerous to pass on – ears and tongues of numerous informers must be guarded against. Just the rumour that Franz Steininger and Anton Guttlein had a radio in their barracks got them tortured and shot.

By April 1945 the International Red Cross had persuaded the wavering camp administration to let them move French, Belgian and Dutch prisoners to Switzerland; a deputy clerk, Hans Marsalek, and his helpers sent out about fifty additional prisoners supplied with false identity papers, in the group of French prisoners. Not all the scheming of the office clerks worked out so successfully, but they persevered, their courage and resourcefulness exceptional, their resolve undimmed.

The Russian prisoners had their minds set on trying to escape, despite reprisals, despite lack of successes. One group included some high-ranking officers, isolated in Block 20 as confirmed escapers or trouble-makers. These were in a most desperate situation, kept on such reduced rations that of the 4,700 officers and prisoners-of-war sent there in March 1944, only 570 were still alive early in February 1945. With nothing to lose, they planned a breakout. Completely isolated, they first set about getting hold of a map of the camp. First they threw slips of paper over the wall separating them from the rest of the camp in hopes an underground organisation would find their appeals for help. It was so. The organisation's members discussed how to assist Block 20. The camp barber's position provided a route. He managed to speak to a Russian officer destined for Block 20 during the routine cutting off of his hair. The barber told him all in Block 20 were listed to be killed, they should make a break for it as soon as possible. The map would be sent to them, fixed to the bottom of a food pail.

The plotters, Lieutenant-Colonel Nikolai Vlasov, Colonels Aleksander Isupov and Kiril Chubchenko and Captain Mardovzov, worked out a ruse to divert the attention of the savage senior block inmate while they tried to find the promised map. On the third day's try, Mardovzov found a pellet pasted on the pail. Scraping it off, he hid it in his mouth. He just had time, later that evening, to pass it on to his comrades. The senior block inmate had observed him, taken his number, and murdered him that same evening. The precious cigarette paper with its map of the camp and its surroundings, had been won, but at great cost. Only days before the escape was due to take place, the other three officer-planners were among a group of twenty-five taken out and shot. The plan went ahead on the revised date of the night of February 1st-2nd. First the senior block inmate was killed by two barracks orderlies. Next an officer addressed the men, who armed themselves with pieces of coal, stones, lumps of soap, two fire extinguishers, boards torn up from the floor. With these pitiful weapons they stormed the front watchtower, ignoring shots fired at them by the SS, retaliating with jets from the extinguishers and a hail of stones that hampered the accuracy of the guards' firing. Blankets from the dead senior block inmate's stockpile, torn into strips, were thrown over the electric fences. Some of the men from the block, about seventy-five of them, already too weak to take part in the escape, had given their clothes to their comrades – perhaps the rags they gave were among the strips of cloth some of those escaping tied round their shoeless feet with bits of string.

At the fence some threw themselves onto the charged wire so that others could climb over their bodies and scale it. Many reached the fields outside the camp. About 500 took part, and 419 got over the fences. Those who remained in Block 20 were killed on the night of the breakout; next morning the area was littered with skeletal bodies dressed in rags, and a mass manhunt began, with the SS, the Wehrmacht, the military and paramilitary units, the Hitler Youth, all, all these brought in – tracking bloody footprints of barefoot people through the snow. The orders went forth, no-one was to be captured, all must be immediately killed. A policeman's report written shortly after the liberation stated that the slush in the street turned red with the blood of those who had been shot. At the nearby town of Muhlviertel, this dreadful event became known locally as the 'Muhlviertel Hare-Hunt.'

But not all of them were caught, not all of them died. Not all who went their struggling way went unhelped, though many of the local population were too frightened to help them, even if they had wished to do so. Of those who were cruel, faced with the eruption of these ghastly, ghostlike figures, who is to know what fear, what urgent instinct of denial, what ancient prejudices activated, led to behaviour hardly believable to the local policeman who made his shocked report on the scenes he witnessed?

The count of those found, and shot on the first day of their flight, was said to be 300. At least they died in freedom.

Only one family, the Langthalers, dared shelter two Russians, but shelter them they did, for three more months, until liberation day came. A very few of the farmers gave food to the scarecrow fugitives. Two other local families, the Mascherbauers and the Wittbergers, gave praiseworthy help. Years later these events were learned about almost by chance. Seven survivors living in the Soviet Union were found and belatedly honoured, years after Stalin's death.

Mauthausen had other sub-camps such as Hinterbruhl. There, in an incident recorded by survivors. a German prisoner, name unknown, refused the order to shoot 150 who were too ill to work. He himself was shot.

Gusen too had its quota of the exceptionally brave. The Austrian kapo in the disinfection section had orders to gas 600 prisoners; he was unwilling, but under threat he passed the order down to subordinates. Marian Molenda, a Pole, knew he could do nothing to save the lives of those six hundred, yet still he would not take part. He said he would rather be killed himself than do it. He was beaten to death by the enraged SS men. His story survives.

Gusen and Steyr Works were both set up for the production of armaments. Slave-labourers worked there, but they did not behave like slaves. Unusable machine guns resulted from the long-term efforts of an Italian team, as Antonio Galiani reported. The Spaniards were not behindhand. Particio Cruz has told how on several occasions they managed to shut the factory down, on one occasion for four days. The tool-setter there, Emil Samek, a Pole, had opportunities for using the skills of his trade. He and others set machines incorrectly, then turned his attention to the stage of final inspection of parts. Wrongly sized parts were passed for assembly, correctly sized ones thrown on the scrap heap. Highly secret as these activities must be, one group of saboteurs might be unaware of the inventive and sophisticated methods used by other groups. Samek did not know until after the war that a group of young Poles used an ingenious method organised by Josef Ladowskii on a tempering facility at the factory to undertake what amounted to 100% sabotage; by not hardening the gun parts properly, the guns would fail after a short period of use. Some Poles gave out damaged implements in the toolhouse, and other Poles used the night hours to substitute defective parts for good ones, the correctly made parts consequently sent back to Steyr to be rectified.

Among civilian workers not averse from joining in acts of sabotage, or helping to protect prisoners from the consequences of large amounts of scrapped parts, were an Austrian civilian called Petrak and a south Tyrolean, Kettner. The Messerschmitt Works, which in 1944 installed a plant to make aeroplane wings, was included in sabotage endeavours – the art of mass-producing unusable parts was further developed there. Skilled workers were required for producing Messerschmitts. Mauthausen's office clerk responded by transferring such men to a sub-camp, so that unskilled workers had to be trained, and they turned out to be remarkably slow on the uptake, and prone to make inexplicable mistakes. The SS made efforts to reduce wasted time, siting the latrines between the workshops – a decision especially appreciated by the Russian rivet-maker, Georgi Aropov. An excellent idea, he thought. As he passed by on his way to take rivets to the assembly workshops, he dropped correctly-sized rivets into the latrine, taking undersized rivets on to the men who used them to make unusable parts. Many prisoners were caught and severely whipped for such tactics; but a Spaniard, Jose Sanz, recalled that when he was suspected of sabotage, he got away with it unpunished because a civilian worker stood up for him.

At the sub-camp Modling, the prisoner-doctors received orders: on March 31st all those considered too weak to march away were to be killed by injecting them with poison. Despite all threats, they refused to do it. No punishments followed – it was never possible to predict how the SS would react.

At Mauthausen in 1944 the task of organising groups to protect prisoners – or even start an uprising – was mooted, with Spanish, French, Russian, Czech, German, Austrian, Yugoslavs and a Polish group set to work, to prepare in precise detail the plans first put forward independently by the ethnic groups.

Such conspiratorial groups experienced the situation differently from those not in the know. A Polish aristocrat, Stefan Badeni, later wrote his memoir. Badeni had been arrested in Hungary, after he had removed himself there with his family when Eastern Poland was occupied. There he had maintained his contacts with the underground movement in Poland, using his high-up connections to aid agents, and counter-signing bills presented for payment by the underground army. His strong Catholic faith seems to have motivated him, in situations doubly strange to someone whose power and privilege had previously led to his only having been spoken to with the most extreme and utmost reverence. This changed somewhat at the first interrogations after his arrest, first as a hostage, then as a suspect.

Many of the Polish landowners in a similar position reserved their greatest hatred for the Russians and despised the Jews. Badeni, while maintaining a definite anti-Soviet position, proceeded from a patriotic and anti-Nazi point of view. His account speaks of opposition to German atrocities, with no signs of anti-Semitism, but a uniquely innocent view of the situation he had landed in, unaware he is singled out for help by unknown comrades, people who seem to know something of this tall, lean, and totally inexperienced prisoner.

With Hungary invaded on March 29th 1944, Badeni was among the first group taken to Gestapo headquarters at the Astoria hotel. In its big underground ballroom, three hundred or so silent, motionless people stood or sat, waiting for interrogation. Next morning, nineteen Hungarians and Badeni were selected out and told they would be killed if there was any sabotage. The novel experience of climbing into a prison wagon followed. After this introduction to a strange new way of life came a shared cell in Fo prison and two interrogations there - unpleasant, but that was all. Yet Badeni was to earn a bitter reproach from the fellow-prisoner, a more worldly-wise young man from Llow, who'd heard him most politely decline the offer of cigarettes made by a visitor, an elderly Count of his acquaintance, on the grounds that he didn't smoke; back in his cell Count Badeni was told, 'You'll never make a prisoner.' Badeni redeemed his reputation by colluding with a fellow-prisoner to ensure that only non-incriminating information would be given by two Poles. Acting as go-between, Badeni learned a long and complicated tissue of lies fit for Gestapo ears, that he could pass on to the next Polish prisoner to be interrogated. His prison education begun, he enjoyed the company of the young people who shared his cell during the weeks that followed. He noted that even some of the guards were not unpleasant, and, still thinking the war would soon end, was not unduly concerned by the bullying behaviour of the SS. Later on, when he learned that the disobedience to orders he showed then, would have meant instant death in a camp, he began to appreciate how well a certain Styrian soldier had protected him during the months in prison.

By August 1944, his account goes, only a few remained in the cell. A soldier would enter, shout out the names he had on a list, telling the named ones to hurry up and get their things together. Then the door banged after them. They had to stand, silent and separate, in the corridor with their faces to the wall, until taken away, to wherever. The usual procedure. On the night of 16th-17th August, Badeni's turn came. Lip-reading from a Jewish prisoner, he found out he would be sent to Mauthausen, his only knowledge of it an impression from the comment of a judge, who had told another prisoner it was beautifully situated, the air was very good there. The journey from Keleti station in cattle trucks got them to Vienna as dusk fell. The trucks shunted backwards and forwards all night, trains were changed, the journey continued. Badeni saw Melk Abbey – unaware that Melk had its satellite camp of Mauthausen, that there too an underground organisation existed. Loiblpass was to him only a station along the way.

More train changes. Then Mauthausen station, followed by standing in the sun for hours, before being formed up into the rows of five that were a regular feature of camp routine. Badeni was tired, already suffering from the effects of malnutrition – he had not eaten the green herbs he thought of as 'weeds' in the prison soup – so in his still-innocent state he was pleased at the first sight of the camp. Entering its gates produced a far different impression. Badeni's memoir mentions that though they were shouted at, they were not beaten; he has no inkling of the struggles and effort of the underground groups in a variety of camps that had brought the regime of 'No beatings', the selflessness of individuals who had firmly declared, 'I don't give beatings'.

Then came their transformation into shaved and ragged prisoners limping along the pebbled way, carrying their SS issue clogs. By good fortune Badeni met with a Hungarian friend, who not only gave him cool water to drink, he explained the time-table of the camp. The kindnesses the Count received, from such people as a young man from Lodz, who saved bits of his own meagre bread ration to buy him shoes, an old man from Konin who helped him at the hardest time, or that man's friend, who wheedled a little extra soup for him, greatly impressed him. And there was a priest who, on Christmas Day, found him from afar, so he could bring to him the word of God. He does not question for himself, how it was, that in that huge camp, the priest found him.

Badeni, luckily recognised by Poles he had been in prison with and Hungarians from his time in Budapest, received good advice from the first, gifts of clothes and soap and a towel by the second, as well as being recommended to the Polish kapo. His beginner's luck held – a handkerchief and a piece of bread and jam, given by a kapo to a new arrival, a 'Zugang', who could only expect the worst treatment! An aristocrat, I would think the value he placed on once more possessing such a civilised article as a handkerchief was considerable. He was weak and ill, but the Polish hospital doctor and the senior block inmate got him to the small hospital headed up by a Czech doctor, and known as The Refuge. Clearly he was known of, for he got the best bed in the best ward. Visitors came, fellow prisoners or patients, even a Russian who invited him to visit him in the Caucasus after the war. Still he had no knowledge of the organisation, as his conversations with a young Pole, who gave him a keen glance and asked him for the story of his imprisonment, showed. This seasoned survivor completed Badeni's education on the rules and conventions of camp life; though not revealing why he now looked better fed and clothed than newcomers, this young man did speak of how he had survived torture after an escape attempt, survived the worst work details, and become resourceful and well-informed on the unwritten laws formed from the co-existence of the prisoners.

By now Badeni was trading cigarettes, giving away some of his bread ration, appearing to know there was an organisation but not knowing what it did. He was either still too frail to be discharged from The Refuge, or else some unknown friend had arranged to keep him there out of harm's way. (He never was allocated to a work detail.) At night he could see the moon as he lay in bed, shining across the barbed wire. One September day, long files of women were to be seen as they passed on their way to barracks – Warsaw's ghostly souls.

Mauthausen was now so seriously overcrowded that sleeping arrangements were unbearable, with four men to every bunk even in the sick-bay. So, when Badeni was moved out of the hospital, the helping hand of yet another prisoner, who got him a sleeping space on a top bunk, again gave him more of a chance to survive. In the bitter winter of January 1945 the roll-call twice each day became an endurance test; early in February, Badeni fainted, a dangerous thing to do. A French friend gave him a hunk of bread as he lay in the hospital corridor, before he was taken on to the larger sick bay. There he got to know about the arriving prisoners evacuated from Auschwitz, Gross-Rosen, and other eastern camps, 7,000 or so who all needed to be squeezed into the already overcrowded hospital. Rations were cut, and cut again. By April there were days when no bread was issued. The extreme of hunger and mental debilitation followed. For those who still lived, there was the alternating hope of liberation and fear of what the camp authorities might do as the end of their rule approached.

All was unpredictable. Allied air-raids were increasing, the sub-camp at Amstetten bombed on March 24th, after which determined women workers sent a deputation of Frenchwomen and one Englishwoman to tell the camp commandant they had decided not to go back to their barracks there at the end of the day's work. How things change – there were no reprisals.

The Polish organisation still helped Badeni; occasional cigarettes, once even a ration of bread were smuggled to him. A surprise event on April 22nd, not known of by Badeni, came with that appearance of a convoy of Red Cross vehicles. 756 women and sixty-seven men were called out, and told they would be taken to Switzerland. For hours, no-one knew whether to believe it, until, after hearing an order in French, they were convinced. Another 596 men, including those smuggled on by the camp committee, went out with a second convoy. After that, with all roads to Switzerland blocked, no more could be sent out. But the convoys had had their effect, the hopes of those who remained were raised, a return home perhaps a possibility.

Hope fell again. The hospital's patients were destined for the gas chambers. The resistance groups did all they could, 378 were saved. Despite their efforts 1,441 were killed between April 21st and the 25th. The definitive act that saved Badeni from being gassed at that time, came in a way he thought mere luck, or a fellow-prisoner's intuition. Badeni relates he was among several hundred of the most feeble patients selected to be sent to a newly-appointed hospital. So they were told. They were promised that there the food ration would be increased – more bread, much more soup. They lined up in their fives, ready to be marched off to the extra soup, the one-sixth of a loaf of bread. A Polish prisoner happened to pass by, looking thoughtfully at the scene. Approaching Badeni, he remarked that, he knew nothing at all, but, he added, he did not like the idea of the new hospital. Did Badeni want to go there?

Badeni did not at all want to go there. The Polish person offered to try to get the clerk to take his name off the list. He was successful, Badeni was allowed to return to his sick-bay barracks. The others marched off. Soon word spread – they had been taken straight to the gas chambers. Later that day, another list of names, but his was not read out. The next day, Sunday, all was quiet. On Monday, the selections started again. This time he was aware of the role of the barracks clerk, who was doing his best to reduce the numbers of those selected, as well as to delay the procedure as much as he possibly could. The risks taken by the clerk who had removed his name from the first selection, after the unknown friend had intervened for him, must have been enormous. That he really was being protected by the organisation is shown by next day's gift to him, a parcel of clothes, in case a quick emergency escape had to be attempted.

Lying in his bunk on May 1st, he overheard a whispered conversation between Germans in the bunk below him. Someone had heard on a radio that the German Army had been ordered to abandon all resistance. Badeni, though now more accomplished as a prisoner, was still not much of a conspirator. He shouted out in Polish what he had just heard as a secret whisper.

Confusion reigned as the SS frantically dismantled the gas chambers and tried to destroy incriminating documents. Food supplies remained at starvation level. The camp management was busy persuading people to join a special unit of the SS as a means of gaining their release. The camp committees were determined that such units would not be used against them. On the 27th the committee had to decide whether to start an uprising in hopes of preventing the death of a group of Upper Austrian communists, thirty-four of them, listed for execution. Eventually they agreed it would be better tactics to provide these men with weapons for their escape. The thirty-four were reluctant to risk an escape in their weakened state, and, with Allied forces expected daily, thought they would not be killed in the camp. They were then advised to hide themselves by going to the hospital section immediately after the morning roll call. Only one man took this advice. The others stayed where they were. They were killed. The resistance decided that the plans made for opposing mass liquidation must be activated.

The Steyr works was their source of weapon supply. Comrades assigned to work there, such as the sabotage expert Ladowski, stole ten machine guns. Missing parts, sketched by other Poles, were made in the workshops. Back in the base camp, Spaniards working in the SS arsenal smuggled in pistols and hand grenades, hiding numerous weapons beneath floorboards in their barracks. Being short of room when a sub-machine gun was brought in, the barber Juan Pages hid it under the floor of the room he was responsible for. Disillusioned SS men gave them weapons, so additional storage space was made under the office floor. Sixteen bottles of petrol were hidden in the barracks wall. Fire extinguishers, for immobilising the watchtower guards, added to the arsenal.

About 8,000 arriving from Auschwitz had amongst them members of their underground organisation. The Austrian veteran Heinrich Durmayer took over the leadership of the international committee, working together with Marsalek and the doughty Kohl. Another International Red Cross convoy arrived on April 28th. Its leader, who had letters of authority, tried to improve the ghastly conditions in the overcrowded camp, in particular the dire sanitary conditions; the food supplies too, which were quite inadequate. As news of Hitler's suicide filtered through, SS men began to pack their bags. Some made a hurried departure. Russian units were advancing east of Mauthausen, but most SS men preferred to surrender to Allied forces approaching from the west. Some, increasingly nervous, even frightened, offered prisoners their help. The Spanish were told, in future they would be treated fairly. SS men even asked not to be harmed. Many got identity cards with false names, and civilian clothes, and were not unwilling to listen to prisoners' suggestions about how some lives could be saved. Despite this, orders from the SS leadership for the killings to proceed were generally obeyed. The majority of the prisoners would know nothing of the anxious work and planning in these last days and hours. From his account, Badeni was probably unaware they were in great danger.

The SS guards left, with the Vienna Fire Brigade as replacements. On May 3rd a prisoner who worked in the jail was ordered to carry the suitcases of the SS out of the camp; the Wehrmacht captain left behind to guard the jail began to cry, and say he was not responsible for the treatment prisoners had there. He was told to give up his pistol and clear out. Then the cells were all unlocked, and the prisoners told they could return to their blocks. That day, no-one did any work. But the replacement guards were still there, the food supply as inadequate as ever.

The international committee decided on action to stop the total disintegration of the camp. Durmayer and Marsalek, as representatives of the committee asked the commandant to turn over the running of the camp to them. There was already much confusion; revenge actions; a Spanish banner that had taken three days to prepare, hung above the main gate, saying that the Spanish anti-Fascists greeted the armies of the liberators; the Fire Brigade still outside the gates; military units of prisoners forming up at various places in the camp, this mixture of events and violent expressions of long-suppressed feelings, needed somehow to be sorted out.

The Red Cross delegate Haeflinger set off hot-foot to Linz, his task to guide American troops to the camp as quickly as possible. These troops reached Gusen first. The degree of self-discipline leading prisoners had created at Mauthausen contrasted with the situation at Gusen. While the main camp's leaders were urging the need for an international committee to stop the chaos, the SS, keen to carry out orders to leave no witnesses, decided to get the prisoners into the tunnel where work was done, on the pretext of an expected air-raid – their real intention to block the entrance and blow the tunnel up. In the meantime the situation remained perilous, with the food supplies plundered and 20,000 still being terrorised by criminal kapos with guns.

Some armband-wearers in senior positions had run away in fear for their lives, others hid in the camp – until the searchers found them. Then lynch law operated, as it did too at Ebensee, when accounts would be squared on May 5th. The SS commandant left, his men replaced by Wehrmacht forces. The officer put in charge of the guards, Captain Alfred Payrleitner, was anti-Nazi. A young Czech, Drahomir Barta, who worked in the office, the camp interpreter, a Yugoslav called Hrvoje Macanovic, the Frenchman Jean Lafitte, the Russian Vladimir Sokolov, had information from Wehrmacht sources, so the prisoners were aware of the intention to kill them on the approach of Allied troops. Payrleitner provided the camp organisation with weapons, Poltrum gave the warning, advising refusal of any order to go into the tunnel.

That same day, May 3rd, the officer-in-charge asked, not ordered, pale and trembling as never before, he asked them to seek protection from gunfire in the tunnel. With the weapons they had been given bolstering their resolve, they decided they would firmly answer, 'No, No!' when their reply had to be given at the morning roll call.

The 10,000 prisoners were lined up. SS men with sub-machine guns stood in a semi-circle behind the block leaders. The officer-in-charge spoke and the interpreter repeated in several languages, they should go into the tunnel. The agreed answer came, 'No!' The officer-in-charge, totally disconcerted, said they need not go into the tunnel if they did not want to, and the SS men left the camp.

At Mauthausen the International Mauthausen Committee openly revealed its function to all the prisoners. Criminal elements were stopped from doing further harm. On the next day at 2.30 p.m. American forces arrived, to be greeted joyously, tumultuously. Their vehicles, the white Red Cross car and two reconnaissance cars, stopped near the hospital section. The gates of the first-aid section were thrown open. With a great shout of joy hundreds on hundreds looking like living dead rushed out to greet their liberators.

The Americans ordered all the guards to assemble and lay down their weapons. Their soldiers did not stay long. Army orders were to continue with reconnaissance work. The leadership of the camp group immediately met to decide what needed to be done, and made necessary arrangements for running the camp. The food storage rooms were put under guard. People were allocated to look after those who were ill.

Durmayer considered that there was still a danger that the SS or the Wehrmacht would return, so he asked Heinrich Kodre to take charge of camp security. In the town an armed group of Spaniards with fighting experience guarded the bridge.

The guard around the camp was well supplied with weapons from the arsenal. At the railway station two truckloads of armed prisoners guarded a carriage containing sugar. German forces crossed the Danube to try to get this sugar, but were defeated in the fight for it that followed. After that lesson, German forces did not attack the camp itself. Precautions against attack were maintained, with all means of transport confiscated and armed units of prisoners sent into the town to organise strategic road blocks, occupy the post office, the Danube bridge and its landing place. By the end of the day, the inmates of the camp felt secure. Information came in throughout the night; committee members wrote it down on forms the SS used for sending messages. Disciplined and efficient, the ex-prisoners were in control. They were also, now, in telephone contact with Gusen.

On May 6th, at 6.30pm, American troop units arrived in strength. The various national committees sent their greetings all over the world. All the camps were now liberated. Three weeks later, Badeni, exhausted in mind and body, was sent over to liberated Gusen, where friendly ex-prisoners cared for him, until both camps gradually emptied. By July he was well enough to be moved to a hospital in Linz. His memoir, a view from a well-disposed though relatively uninformed individual, reveals something of the unknown debts that many ex-prisoners must owe to the named and unnamed, the dead and the living who attained their full humanity in the passing on of a word of hope, a crust of bread, a civilian suit of clothes, a handkerchief. Let us hope the future becomes in time the future of their wish.

QUESTIONS – AND ANSWERS?

My knee – ouch, giving me gyp as usual. Crunch-crunch I go up the gravel to my front door. Hello, there's my phone, ringing, ringing. Door needs a push to open.

The place smells damp, that phone, shrill now. Cross the hall. The slippery coldness of the phone. The tinny quack, a woman's voice – 'Mr. Milne?' Immediately I know. A knowledge that floods my mind. Grabbing for pen and pad, I note down the ward number. Open visiting, says the quacking voice.

I don't like answerphones, who does, but I must leave messages, for Jane, for Simon. Just in case, I shove the manuscript in a bag. At the door, I dash back for a couple of clean handkerchiefs for him. Fresh from the wash. Wholesome.

Weighed down with all these typewritten pages, quick as I can trudge up the drive to the hospital. It's a funny thing to find out, knowledge can be a weight, heavy as a rock or a load of topsoil. I'll tell him, I've tried my best, put in the names I got to know of. The long hard slog researching, uneasily aware, many equally worthy of remembrance are missing from the histories, the stories and snatches of stories. So many diaries, so many many memoirs, the need in pain-filled indignant words; the tales told with their heart's blood, but heard? Really heard I mean?

The hospital. Not distinguished looking. Parked ambulances. Whiffs of antiseptics haunting the polished-floor walkways. The usual lettering on signs with arrows, with the corridors to trek along intersected as usual by corridors equally straight, equally long, equally hung with paintings by local artists supposedly cheering to anxious people looking for their outpatient's clinics, or visitors like me seeking the in-patients up the stairs, through the swing doors, an open-doored labelled room.

A side-ward, just one bed in it. Antiseptic odour, plus – a pervasive mingling of ambiguous smells not quite suppressed, appalling half-sweet signals of approaching death. The shallow mound of bedcovers shifts at my approach, the propped-up figure in the bed sketches a gesture with a stick-insect hand.

'Hello, Mr. Julius.' I force out a cheerful voice, plump myself down in the chair he's indicated. Pointlessly I ask him how he feels, he looks as near a ghost as makes no matter. His eyes still glitter. I fumble out my thick typescript. His leathery experiment at a hand, something escaped from an old-fashioned film, the mummy's hand or some such, shakes as its skewed fingers reach out.

I hear the scratch of his nails on the plastic cover I'd fitted my book into. His eyebrows rise in a mute question. I tell him, I've done as best I can with it.

'To do one's best, a book – precious lifeblood … that is all anyone can do.' He's too weak to gasp out more. His face, his pleasure at the clean handkerchiefs. We sit in silence a long time. Lost in thinking. I stop my eyes from drooping shut. If you sleep well, the night is short. I've had long nights since I got myself involved. Neuengamme's end, that gave me one of the longest, before I could make myself write down what happened there, but then I thought, come on now, don't deny them, it would be damnable to deny them, to use the power of denial to wipe out the memory, seven chaps trying against the odds to save their mates, drowning in the icy waters of the bay.

Mr. Julius half-slumbers. From time to time a nurse peeps in at us. The rattle of the tea-trolley coming round. I begin to speak, half to Mr Julius and half to myself, just telling a tale:

'1999, what a year. From May to December, I took to visiting libraries – visiting? I haunted them. Librarians got to recognise me, helped me find books, then sometimes I found things out, in books I hadn't been looking for. Sometimes – drawing a blank. Not to mention the agonies I went through, trying not to make a twit of myself struggling with horribly worded instructions on how to use the Internet, wondering if my poor plants were wilting while I was away from home.

'I got back lugging two see-through plastic folders, the shiny sort, stuffed with notes, not at all as orderly as I'd meant to make them. It took me a good while to get the hang of taking notes from books, at least the notion of it was something useful left over from school. Then it was Christmas. Not much of a time when there's no children to wake you up before you want to be woken up on the morning, excitement bursting out of them, spouting out like water from a fountain you forgot to switch off – but Mr. Julius, I don't think I ever had the makings of a married man.

'Then the New Year. The Millennium New Year. The village put on a special show for the Millennium. A street party, fireworks, that sort of thing. In the usual way, Mr. Julius, I spend New Year's Eve at home, slippers on, fire glowing, enjoying a generously filled glass of an especially fine single malt whisky, splendidly golden, showing at its best in my one remaining item from the cut-glass whisky set. A glass of good malt, my one luxury. Courtesy of Angus, of course, I couldn't still do it if he hadn't left me … what he did. Angus was always the bold one out of the two of us, or maybe I was exceptionally timid, hung back too much, didn't dare. Nobody these days would turn a hair.

'I got to wondering what it'd be like to join in with the celebrations. The sky had cleared, it shone stars. A mile and a half to the village, not a long walk for a healthy man, not if you've got a warm coat to wear. Not like… you know.

'A builder's van parked sideways across the road – an improvised stage. The crowd, mainly youngsters, teenage girls determined not to look cold in thin wisps of dresses. Glazed and smiling upturned faces. The singer, transforming the banal words of an undistinguished tune, belting it out with all she could give. Quite a good voice, that's what I told myself in excuse for – being excessively moved. I'd been reading about the camp orchestra, how the woman prisoner put in charge got obsessed with the need to play the violin as beautifully, as correctly, as ever she could. And the listening prisoners, they felt – not as they felt on the long hard days without the music.

'Before I started all the research, Mr. Julius, I didn't so much as know how to spell Auschwitz; come to that, I didn't even know for sure that it's in Poland. Now I've laid out the ground, ready for seeds to grow.

'As I was saying, with still half-an-hour to midnight, colder, the crowd bigger, families together, little children wrapped up warm. One little fellow, only about two, perched up on his dad's shoulders, his two fat hands clutching dad for safety. Dad held on to the child's legs and jigged about, wordlessly telling the child, This is how you dance. Then someone else, a relation, or maybe he was a family friend, felt one of those fat little hands, pulled off one of his own big gauntlets and tried to fit it over the child's wee hand. Tried to. But what the child wanted was the safety of grasping dad tight. One of the children in the newspaper photograph, I daresay too weak to stand, clinging to a woman, she holds him as a mother holds her child. Wrapped up in a blanket, he was.

'At the back of the crowd it was darker and more of us oldies stood about chatting. Not wanting to break into conversations, not knowing what would be the right thing to say anyway, I stayed on the shadowy verge. Countdown to midnight, 6,5,4,3,2,1, and a great shout as everyone raised their hands, turned to each other, Auld Lang Syne, Happy New Year! I'd joined in, really joined in, part of it all although I'd gone there alone. Yes, I forgot the awkward shyness that makes it hard for me to talk like I'm talking to you, not hiding my feelings, I mean.'

Expressions come and go over the old man's face, just a gleam of eye showing as his lids flicker. With an effort he speaks.

'Photographs too, drawings, paintings, each a life risked to pass on from ghetto and prison, camp and village street this knowledge, the hope beyond it. Perhaps you know, Mahler's widow rescued his last Symphony, unfinished, struggled up the goat paths and across the mountain pass with that musical manuscript under her arm: Mahler's last work, and though it fades away as if to nothingness, all is not lost, it passes through, through, reaches that otherness we sometimes glimpse beyond the horror … as with – the ending of a book "Dr. Faustus" – in near-despair – despite all doubt – yes, the precious lifeblood of a master spirit. In a strange land.'

A gasping pause, he strains to say more. Before he gains breath for it, I hear footsteps, dull and click-clack ones, that tell me two people hurry along the corridor. A nurse brings two more chairs.

'Is it alright for us all to stay?' Jane's asking. The nurse nods: "It's guid the wee mannie has his family roond him."

We speak together in hushed voices. Jane inches her chair away from Simon's, they avoid looking at each other, Mr. Julius' eyes move under shut lids. His breathing, a struggling unrhythm to it. I hold my own breath until his gets started again.

Simon's bony face more stretched than ever, his extra-large adam's apple leaps as he swallows hard. Thin wisps of gingery hair, clung damply to his lumpy skull. Mr. Julius raises a hand, murmurs a welcome, even twitches his lips into a ghost of his sardonic smile. Simon clears his throat, gripped by the need to speak: 'I heard this story about a painter,' he says, 'A Bavarian chap. Johannes Koetz Mateuz. A portrait painter, famous, in the early thirties, asked to paint Hitler's portrait. He refused, he was a pacifist. He got to England, a refugee – brought out with him what he valued most, his master work, a huge painting, a personal manifesto as it were; and he had it cut to pieces. When I think about my grandfather, my uncle – I think about young Germans who wouldn't have heard anything but propaganda, they'd believe it, swallow it down not knowing mental poison when they got the taste of it. Hitler Youth, schooled in Hitler schools, fed on Hitler bullshit. When German people saw chained prisoners being marched along to the daily work in the factories or the quarries, Grandfather said they'd either look indifferent or sneer hatefully, no-one showed pity or regret – in Poland, prisoners might find little parcels of food left for them. Only not very often if they were thought to be Jews.'

Simon struggles to keep his voice steady, he twists the corner of his handkerchief between thumb and first finger:

'Jews put up a good fight in the ghettos, Mr. Julius, in lots of ghettos. And with the partisans. Or, the four hundred craftsmen from Lutsk with their weapons ready when Ukrainian auxiliary police came, with orders to take them away. They couldn't win, they knew that, they died as their workshops went up in flames.'

My thoughts run in parallel, pervaded with a sense of – of what I can't just describe. Shame, I think, as I add, 'Some of us have said, we didn't know over here what was going on over there; how come, when as far back as September 19th 1933 'The Times' reported the goings-on at Orianenberg Concentration Camp, prisoners forced to stand to attention three hours at a time, hardly any food, beatings ... and all the smuggled-out truths of it – the Allied troops, when they liberated the camps at the end of the war, weren't impressed by the local inhabitants' attitudes either. How many claimed not to know what all that black smoke meant? None of us are free of blame or responsibility for our blindnesses and deafnesses. The other day, I was listening to the radio, not knowing the talk I had on had anything to do with the camps. A woman novelist was talking about Primo Levi's book, 'If This is a Man.' She was saying, she'd only just brought herself to read it, she'd thought it would be too awful to read about all the things he'd been through, and she was so surprised, when he worked at the Buna plant, there'd been secretaries walking about – in her words powdering their noses – and she'd said, her words, that until the moment she'd read that, she hadn't realised there were so many collaborators about. Collaborators! What's that supposed to mean, weren't we all collaborators who looked or didn't look at the newsreels and did or didn't know about the torrents of books telling the unimaginable – and if it's been hard for me to write, worried it'll sound too depressing for comfortable people to want to read it, well what that woman says shows me, if I thought I was ignorant, there's worse than me in the world, so there is a need to spell it out, tell what real men and women did.'

The manuscript stares up from the hospital bed-cover. Simon's not likely to think much of my writing style, I don't suppose he's much of a gardener come to that. And Jane? She'll find something to say that doesn't hurt my feelings, and yet it won't be what she doesn't think either.

'You're a romantic,' Simon told me, when we met up that second time. I'd had to get to the University, find the Library there, and then the cafeteria. I told him, 'There's a saying, chance is a fine thing. Primo Levi, he wrote about chance, and about small causes. His friend Alberto had scarlet fever as a child. Primo hadn't. Near the end Primo Levi went down with fever, he was in the infirmary while Alberto was marched away on the deathly evacuation. By that chance, Primo Levi survived. By chance, Hermann Langbein survived, transferred before the escape attempt that cost Ernst Burger his life.

I read a book once, where a seaman sat on deck weaving matting. He sits there meditating on life's weaving together of fate, necessity and chance. The seaman had a mad captain, they were chasing a white whale, it caught up with them at the end. But as chance had it, this seaman had fallen overboard a few days before, so although the ship goes down with all hands, he was the one survivor left to tell the tale. The unlucky chance of that big wave seamen call a lump of water, that came for Angus as he reached out to secure the line. Lost overboard. My thoughts keep wandering to Angus, brother of my heart, the romantic of the family though hardly anyone would guess that about a north-east fisherman. His love affair with the sea, his belief he knew its moods so well he was safe whatever the storm was like. Most of the time, he was right, he didn't behave as chancily as most folk thought, not really. If it hadn't been for that fault in the trawl door … Or if he could have reached to attach the chain … They had families to feed, he took the chance of leaning overboard without a line. The lump of water broke his hold. The skipper caught sight of a yellow oilskin in the water. Did the correct thing, then. A Williamson Turn, 180 degrees around, get the boat back to Angus.

The chance of rain, me in the café, when you strolled in. The chance that Simon and Jane came along to hear me. Chance when plants mutate, chance and the environment. Chance and the environment and time. Time's changes responsible for differences in appearance amongst us, us the human race. Superficial differences. Our genes much of a muchness. That's not just something I learned when I was reading up on horticulture, it was what my parents explained to me, when they told me, I'd been asking them why they'd given my brother and me names both starting with A, and mum smiled and said, we didn't want to change the name you brought with you as a tiny baby, Arthur, your birth mother couldn't keep you so we brought you up as ours and so you are.

And I'd never even guessed. Why do I think of Angus now? It's that Williamson Turn thing, the technique for performing an otherwise impossible manoeuvre. After I met you, Mr. Julius, that's when I made my own Williamson Turn. To go back, to the time before timidity stopped me doing anything with my life. Luckily I've always been a reader, so it didn't come as hard as it might, to read and find things out. Simon can rattle on about how all State power's oppressive, the Nazis just carried it to the limits of its conception, power concentrated, and we never think about how State Power is grinding us down too. Simon says that although a lot of students don't get a buzz from political philosophy, he reckons that through his Jewish grandfather, he's inherited a sort of intellectual opposition, the refusal to be intimidated by the idea of being different; he accepts his difference, his sense of standing on the edge of society and dissecting its foibles, like all the Jewish stand-up comedians that take the mickey, it's Jews who invented alternative comedy, perhaps it's because we couldn't stand the idea of any more tragedy we've turned to satire, to joking. So Simon says.

I did tell him about what happened to Angus, how close we'd been, how Angus was the only one from my young days who hadn't teased me about me stopping in to read a book instead of going out to the monkey run to meet a girl, maybe Angus understood what I was timid about.

Jane, suddenly talkative. Reminiscing. Her childhood fascination with her father's round, shiny fob watch in the pocket of his navy-blue waistcoat. Jane telling us, when she was very little, she almost, perhaps really did believe the watch was a live thing, a sort of pet, that lived in his pocket, called, my-railway-watch. Railwaymen had to have accurate watches just as they had to have books of rules – the difference it made, having rule books and timetables and good time-keeping watches brought in when the railways were built and time was standardised across the country. People from the country, like his father's father, came in to live in the towns then had to get used to moment-to-moment time-keeping in the factories and the mills where you had a number and you had to clock in each morning and each afternoon with a numbered time card. After forty-odd years of scratting you'd be all at sea when you weren't needed anymore. Drifting. No sense of direction, something missing so you didn't know which way to go. Angus told me, how before anyone worked out a tremendously difficult clock so you knew your longitude out at sea, you didn't know whatever-which-way to go, you had to sail by God and by guess, swept onto the rocks as like as not. And he reckoned that Harrison making that clock seeded the future, led to England hoisting the flag around the world; new frontiers, rich pickings. It didn't stop there.

'My grandmother,' says Jane, 'Used to scrub the washing every Monday with a dolly on the side of the tub, and now my mother's wondering what sort of a two-piece she should order off the Internet and wear when she comes to my graduation ceremony next year.'

Jane's a nice girl, she's got a kind face, but well I don't know, it's hard to make youngsters out. Or families, come to that. Strange things, families. The three of us have been elevated to be Mr Julius' family. We talk on, the way you do when you pass the time of waiting. Is it to him we speak, or to each other, or maybe to ourselves? I remember, as a child, I'd sat in a forest and watched the wood ants streaming to and fro tugging improbably large-looking bits of twig or whatever to their nests. In uncountable numbers. And then another ant-hill, and another. All the camps, a dense network spread like a vast gripping octopus over Germany, over the occupied countries, servicing the German industrial firms to keep the system trundling on. Slave workers' numbers rounded up or rounded down, faces that make up the numbers momently changing – how to represent the truth of the minds that persisted in being minds, making it possible for us to learn at least something of what happened? Could Simon help with that? He's very quiet, thinking his own thoughts I suppose.

* * *

Arthur looks – Arthur looks as if he's trying to work something out. He wants answers, like the answers to sums in the back of a school textbook. He puzzles his head for explanations, looks things up to find definitions. As if a dictionary definition will beam down a searchlight of understanding. Or, he thinks, he can get at some convincing explanation through telling himself stories, he can get at truth through those stories he tells himself. I'm looking for deeper levels of explanation, variegated truths... truths I choose because they suit me? We do that, I think, because it calms us in the fragile turbulence of existence in a world we can't understand.

Why can't we? We need to have full information to know the truth of any event. Grandfather used to shrug aside questions about the truth of what happened – he'd paradoxically say, no-one knew, because only everybody could know the truth. A shrug of the shoulders, Grandfather's contribution, as if to say, with so many gone we cannot know truth. Goethe said, only everybody could know the truth. And here I am, stuck with the uncertainty of the unverifiable, in perpetual doubt.

Does logic do nothing to help me with the problem of explaining the Nazi era? Or our present era? Or settle my doubts of our species' fitness, in the Darwinian sense, to survive? Could it be that most people just didn't think? How unlikely that seems. And yet, in America, that physicist, Feynman, no slouch he, willingly working on making the atom bomb, because he thought it would be bad if the Nazis made it first; and he didn't stop to consider circumstances had changed while he and his fellow scientists were still utterly absorbed in making the thing work, and when it worked, when Hiroshima frizzled and fried, Feynman sat on the front of a truck, drunk, and played the bongo drums. Later, he said he just didn't think. In the grip of buzz from a successful experiment. I daresay Werner Von Braun got his buzz too.

Historical factors, the social situation, protective psychological devices we use, thrown into the recipe, like adding milk and eggs to a cake, like the seed cake my mother used to make when I was a little boy, me wriggling about on the seat of the wooden kitchen chair with rails that stuck into your back when you leaned against them for more than a minute or two; not that I'd sit still long enough for that, and mother saying the seat would be well polished by the time the cake got mixed, stirred all up together ready to put into the oven, hey presto, seeds sprinkled onto the top, baked into a whole, a recognisable, usable, nameable object. Grandfather used to pick up the crumbs, even the very little ones, on the tip of his first finger, plodge, plodge, carefully transfer each speck to his mouth. Crumbs of cake for him, crumbs of knowledge for me.

The recipe tells you how to do it. The glorious smell of it baking told you it was coming on the way it should. The why of it remains obscure. I can't accept as explanation, only the how of what took place. My grandfather couldn't. It tormented him to the end. It torments me now. I need to see deeper, why? Why not stay with the surface practicalities of life, question nothing – or would that be to make of myself a mental Musselman? There is that within me it would be well to suppress. When I nearly hit Jane while we were arguing, I recognised that; by her shocked look, the way she let her hair fall over her eyes so I wouldn't see her mind's hurt… Take another route. Look for the best in people. Go on from there. Learn if there's something to wish for.

*   *   *

Dozing off in the chair. In the half-dark. I hardly ever remember my dreams, but starting up awake I just caught sight of him before I'd come right round. The yellow oilskin gleaming, rain running down it in wiggly streaks. His face all wet too. A lock of hair plastered over his forehead, darkened to mud-colour. But smiling. And I realised, I've had dreams like it before, that I must have forgotten when I woke up.

Forgetting, that gets to be a problem for us. It's a burden to my mind, the episodes I know I've missed out or names I can't remember, hard as I've tried to add each to the roll call of honour. If that's not a too old-fashioned way to think about it. The least I can do, by way of recognition. Their names, hopes, deeds.

There was that chap I met in a pub, he'd had a few I think. Or maybe it was me who'd had a few. He was Irish, definitely, and we got talking. I don't exactly remember how we got onto Ireland. But he told me a lot of things I didn't know, and when he was on about the Black and Tans, he said that in County Cork, where he came from himself, there'd been an awful massacre, and that the names of those Irish people killed by the Black and Tans were all written down, with a little bit about each of their lives. And I thought then, if I could do something like that, then the work of it would be worthwhile. Doing it worthwhile would be good enough for me, I don't have delusions of grandeur like that old chap Faust we read about when I was a kid at school.

Yes, it was his old smile. He raised his hand, waved to me, walking backwards – no, not walking, his feet weren't moving. He just, went backward, gliding away across the sea's surface. When he saw I looked at him, knew him, of course I knew it was Angus, he didn't wave again, his arm dropped. But then as he got further and further away, he gave me a thumbs-up sign. He might have been going to say something, it was when I leaned forward straining to try and make out what he said that my leg jerked and I woke up, woke up before he could tell me what he wanted to say.

Perhaps he meant me to know – to know what, that it's over now, task done? It's been a lot of work. Time, now, to get back to the only thing I'm any good at. But even if I had the dosh, which I don't, I wouldn't want to go back to the landscape gardening. Jane's idea – as she said, so many more people these days are interested in healthy eating, makes it tasty too, using herbs. So if I grew them organic, and I know I could, I could build up a market stall or something, a way of selling without ripping people off. Just allow enough of a margin to keep the growing going.

Arthur, my lad, that's the way to do it. Mr Julius, I'll try to tell you when you open your eyes, you might think it's a healthy occupation for a chap like me who's not a hero, wouldn't have worn a red armband in a camp – maybe a pink triangle if I'd been a bit more daring – but would like to feel in some small way he's been some use in the world. I'd like to think, that young railwayman, Karel, he wouldn't think too badly of me. Lots of ordinary people like him took risks, did their duty, no, that's not right, they chose to do it. Chose to; I choose. What have I learned from all this, not just facts figures dates impossible names, not just typing with two fingers instead of the one, what have I learned for myself?

If I've learned anything worth knowing, it's not to let myself be bullied into not doing the things that seem right for me. I think that's something worth knowing, don't you, Mr. Julius?

*   *   *

Mr Julius, Arthur blushed like a beetroot – organic of course – when I kissed him, and what d'you know, Simon chortled, positively chortled. Arthur's made up his mind, he knows where he's going. And Simon?

Simon's been looking wretchedly tired, lately. Now he has his degree – not the First he'd hoped for, but an Upper Second is good enough to do research – he's thinking about a PhD topic. Simon will take to research, it's more him than first degree work. It's me who's become terminally unsure. Can I go on with the Law degree? I went into it, let's face it, not with any great enthusiasm, but, a career, well-paid, not questionable like financial services – and yes, underneath the practicalities, with a belief, innocent in its nature, in the great equation, Law = Justice = Fairness. A romantic illusion, inherited from my mother and fostered by naff TV series that I brought with me into a degree course that isn't about what I thought it would be about. A future that I don't know if I want, like working for a big firm in the City.

What's international law? A body of moral principles, I assumed, accepted as valid by those whose job it is to ratify treaties. E.g. the 1907 Hague Convention, with its clauses about the dictates of public conscience. The laws of humanity. The Nuremberg Trials laws, devised to bring war criminals to justice and deter nations from getting up to similar mayhem on future occasions. But then I studied up on how law for the Nuremberg Trials was decided on. First, the question of bombing, the destruction of cities complete with their citizens. In the Second World War, both sides did it. Both, ruthlessly. Therefore, since both had done murder, it wasn't regarded as a suitable theme for inclusion in new laws designed to deter nations from doing it again. Not at Nuremberg not at Tokyo was the issue of aerial bombardment so much as put on the agenda as a possible war crime.

Likewise the Naval Criminal Law Acts. German admirals were charged after the war with violating the London Naval Treaty of 1930. And got clean off, on the undeniable grounds that they had done nothing at all more than the Allies had done. An irrefutable argument, in the legal terms the lawyers decided on – criminal acts at the Nuremberg Tribunal defined as and confined to: those committed by a defeated enemy who planned and performed aggressive acts not performed likewise by the conquering army.

The attempt to indict some of the camp doctors who did experiments – though not the professors who supervised their so-called science – fell flat on its face when defence lawyers argued that the camp experiments were only the equivalent of malaria experiments done in America in 1945. So although a new code was hastily put together, hundreds got US citizenship, professors got highly respectable careers at the School of Aviation Medicine, repeating and expanding experiments based on what was done at Dachau, Barracks 5, a low-pressure chamber installed handily next to the hospital - set up hand in glove with the Luftwaffe, who wanted information on altitude sickness in high-speed flying. All fully sanctioned by the overseeing Institute in Berlin. Etc. The experiments on twins. Sterilisations. Block 10 at Ravensbrück, injections of caustic chemicals to seal women's fallopian tubes. The infected wounds …Oh yes, I've done my bit of research too; doing the experiments was a career opportunity for doctors, who only had to join the SS to climb that ladder. And I'd believed that in the eyes of those who make and administer the law – two wrongs don't make a right. I'd thought, laws are to protect innocent people, not a tool to let powerful people get away with their crimes, even add to their power.

Simon sighed when I told him, he sees consequences in a flash, he said, you've only one more year to do, why not go on and get your degree? He wasn't entirely pleased when I said, did he mean, not bother about how the laws work, who they work for? We had – words. But I didn't want to row with him, I switched off that particular conversation. So I'm having this conversation with myself. Or with you, Mr. Julius, are you listening as you lie there getting near and nearer to the time of peacefulness for yourself, your time of not having to make an effort for anyone anymore?

I could get my degree. With a job I'd soon have a flat, a car, nice life-style, go clubbing when I liked. I might even do something useful, giving legal advice or taking up cases of injustice. But. Even if I got the cases I wanted, I'd still have the weight of the established system bearing down, eroding me.

Duplicity. The multiplicity of little, little-by-little acts of indifference or meanness or hurt sucked in those well-meaning people who'd make excuses to themselves, justify murder, be good fathers, kind dog-owners. We all like to think of ourselves as good people. When we say the guards were evil men, some considerably more evil than others, such a convenient way of separating ourselves from what they did, of assuring ourselves, oh no, of course we couldn't do anything like that, we have no dark shadow within ourselves.

The first guards had been nobodies in their ordinary lives, common criminals given the chance of not being held to account for brutality or stealing the rations. Getting power over a hut full of powerless men – at long last somebodies, and hooked on it. They'd be judge, they'd be jury. Hooked on power, comes the moment you need another fix. And another. And the next one a tad stronger, and so it goes on. Carrying out Himmler's orders without making any connections between that and what they did in the other parts of their lives. Little by little, a person's downward road; unseen, a price to pay, depersonalisation, our lives stored in little boxes, so much left-over damage, damage to so many. I haven't thought such weary thoughts before. I used to think, Great, I'll make loads of money, I'll power dress, wear a sharp suit to work, keep slim with a weekly workout at the health club, design myself – as the professional young woman, self-aware, self-possessed, self-created. Enjoying the good life of anything goes as long as it's getting and spending money. Enjoy! What else is there to do, these days?

Simon talks a lot about freedom, people need the freedom to make their own mistakes. He had such a hard time when he was at school. So analytical, so systematic, he has reason to be utterly wary, questioning rules, structures, hierarchies. His uncle, his grandfather. Simon carries the residual damage.

My own father, bound to his timetable, monitored by the round face and shiny surround of his reliable time-synchronised railway watch. A sign, the resonance of depersonalisation symbolically triggered in ourselves by an impersonalised society, whereas a natural set-up takes its time from the changing seasons. But he was happier then than he would be now, and better respected, in those days every little boy wanted to grow up to be an engine driver. That's gone now, pushed aside with the sweep of a handbag. The Railway Timetable, a sick joke.

Simon's bony knees, his sleepless nights, his bitten-down fingernails – philosophy's got its points, but I reckon people's feelings are more important when push comes to shove. That's what I was thinking about, trying to sort my muddles out, last night, in the middle of the night, Simon asleep, his breathing slower and deeper than when he's only pretending and I lay wide awake thinking. So many times, quite ordinary people helped someone trying to escape. A woman cleaner, Annie Noack, in an office stole an official stamp. Or, the woman who let an escapee hide in her apartment. The man who bathed their wounds. That old brute of a convict, who wouldn't, no he would not, beat the prisoners he'd been ordered to punish. Else, the prostitute who wouldn't whip another woman. The non-aligned ordinary ones who chose to risk their own existence – to protect a stranger.

Sometimes they didn't consider it a choice. Karel the railwayman said, it was his duty. For the Nazis, duty meant doing as you were told. But for those like Karel? The experience of duty for him was choosing to stick by his notion of right, as a duty to himself. He wouldn't have bad dreams in the middle of the night. According to Simon duty is a concept that came in, for us, with the railwayman's rule-book. He thinks the Industrial Revolution happened, in England, instead of the other sort, because it was funded by money from the Slave Trade, and so England could go on to have the Empire, with the Scots as junior partners in the British Empire Firm. That's what Simon says. He says you have to take a world view, if it hadn't been for the Stock Market crash in the United Snakes then they wouldn't have stopped funding Germany with more money than their annual War Reparations costs, and then there wouldn't have been economic crisis for the Weimar Republic, and so on. If there hadn't been that, there wouldn't be this. The sum of our past, present, future choices. For us now, the sum of the eighties, the nineties, the new century's neuroses accumulated in the time when individualism appeared to negate even the notion of society?

Mr. Julius, last night I lay there, just thinking: alright, how does a person decide what hurts, what hinders or helps and heals. So much need of healing, so little we do about it. Thinking, in the middle of the night. The choice made in the forest of the night, and not to be forgotten, nor pushed aside in the hurry of the day. To learn how to remember our humanity, be aware, in the humdrum, in the banal and usual of our everyday lives, that a look, a word, is allowed us. Easy acts, difficult ones sometimes, that re-inforce our own dignity - and bring recognition to the dignity that inheres in the known and unknown other.

Mr Julius, do you think I should go on with studying Law, the way I'm seeing things now? If I was floundering and couldn't help him, Simon would fall apart, splinter into a thousand pieces. Or, if I do find my way, our ways must still diverge. His path is a different one. There's a chill breeze coming from him right now.

I could take a year off. Backpack about the world. Voluntary service overseas. I must make my mind up, one way or the other. How, when public opinion as received wisdom gets spun and unspun, look how we've veered, veneered truth, revered the grab-alls, the what's-in-it-for-me brigade – how would I know what's what? Ordinary common-sense, unquestioned assumptions, of questionable validity. Power lies elsewhere than where it seems, propelling obscure purposes that would wake us up at night screaming if we knew what they might lead to.

That woman – Else – retained a feeling of what she wanted to do, I think she would not let herself be numbed into indifference, the disregard of feeling. Whatever her reasons for refusing the order to whip another woman, that's not the important thing. What I want to get at is her feeling, the deep-down feeling that underlies thought, that frames thought before it rises to the surface of the mind dressed up in words. That's how I understand things. I'm not a heroine. I'm not a throwback to the sixties. I wouldn't go on marches like my mother. I'm not Sister Hannah, who carried the banner. That was my mother's mother's generation. I'm stuck with this feeling, I go round and round in my mind and I don't know what to do, I'm stuck. My mind's like a mud patch, all my ideas stuck and trapped in mud. I feel like stopping any and everyone who happens along. Stopping them, asking them, What should I do? What should I do? What would you do?

*   *   *

What would I do? Ah, my dear, my time of choices is now in the past. My speaking now is only possible within my head – but it is a pleasure, that lying here, I hear you, your thoughts not needing the disguises that words may put around them to cloak their meanings. Perhaps in this way you will eventually become clear to yourselves, though of course you and Simon do not as yet understand each other very well, that is not yet possible. But the process begins, your minds have been picked up by the scruff of the neck and thoroughly shaken, the protective falsehoods stripped away, your thoughts will settle down again in places different from where they were before. Painful, painful!

Jane, it would pain you if you knew a use that Landsberg jail was put to after the war was said to have ended. You have heard of that jail in Bavaria, it was there that Hitler had been held in 1923, that is right, where he wrote 'Mein Kampf.' So, his favourite industrialists such as Alfred Krupp – you may remember, the prisoners working in his arms factories sent out messages to the Allies, bomb the Krupps Works, even though we are slave labourers there – Herr Krupp also had an excellent time of it at Landsberg, an elite prisoner, holding board meetings in a room put aside for him, he and his like leaving their cells at will, with access to their bank accounts. Germany might be starving; their diet, such delicacies as caviar and champagne. Not, however, for those scientists of much eminence who devised the V1, the V2 rockets worked on by the slaves at Dora. For the clever scientists, there were the aeroplanes to take them to the American research institutes where their talents could contribute to nuclear weapons being devised there. Nerve gases too. Did Arthur discover that in the camps the Allies found bombs filled with nerve gases, and of these many were taken to England, to Porton Down where their uses were developed, tested on British soldiers?

Not all the prominent Nazis were so useful, many in Landsberg appreciated the Spanish lessons which would help them settle into new lives in South America. It is said that those who knew well of matters in the Soviet Union – and there were many of them, with heavy crimes to answer for – these criminals instead of being tried were without delay recruited to work for the CIA. Those major criminals tried post-war, only 22 selected ones, allowed to go into court dressed up in clothes of their own choosing; some of them, possibly Himmler even, faked their suicide and went – who knows where. Jane, many people will turn away from such knowledge, but you do not convince me you will be one who makes such a decision.

Simon, your mind warns you well of what wriggles within you, the same worm that wriggles deep within each of us, even within those who after their own dreadful suffering felt the overweening wish to find a place for themselves. To be aware of the danger, that is in the first place necessary for us not to take the path so sunny looking in the light of our good intentions, that would in reality blast destruction on the hopes, the dreams of the future of those we should regard as brothers, as sisters.

Though you think I sleep, death is not yet. Not quite yet. Arthur will sit with me through this last night.

If I could speak to you, Arthur, I would relate to you the tale of Benzion Rappoport, not without resemblance to your own case. This man, once upon a time a teacher in Cracow, as he was taken on the cattle-truck train to Belzec, going through Poland he manages to throw something into a field. This something picked up by a man, a Polish peasant. And what is it this Polish peasant has found? It is an exercise book, covered page on page in Hebrew writing – which he does not understand. But on the outside of this bundle of papers, a scrap of paper scrawled on in Polish writing, and this he does manage to read. He makes it out, it says, 'Pious soul, this is a man's life work. Give it into good hands.'

The peasant hides the writings away. When the war is over, he takes a train to

Warsaw, he stands about looking, perhaps as I have looked into the faces of strangers, as I looked once into yours. He seeks for someone who looks like a Jew. There are not many Jews to be seen in Warsaw, 90% of Polish Jews are perished.

At last, in the lobby of a hotel, the Hotel Polonia, he sees two men among the crowd, who recognise each other, who embrace. The Polish peasant hesitates, then making up his mind he speaks to them. 'You are Jews?' he asks. 'Yes, indeed we are' they answer. He draws out the packet of papers, the ink faded now. The two Jews – by a strange chance as children they were taught by this same Benzion whose legacy they hold now in their hands – they read, here is expounded Hegel, here is Kant, Schopenhauer, famed German philosophers whom the death-train man had thought deeply upon. Also there are his own thoughts on ethics, on religion, on the methods of scientific enquiry; delivered up to these two survivors, by this 'pious soul'.

If my voice still served my wish, I would say to you, Arthur my friend, while Jane and Simon go out to the world, perhaps hand-in-hand, your life's work as a man is achieved, you must seek a pious soul to receive your book. To spread its seeds, its philosophy, as the teacher's pupils who published his essays did for Benzion, who though perished at Belzec, had his wish for the truths of his life's work to survive.

Jane, you and Simon, may build a good life together yet, children as you are of the future of the wish. You should get to know each other. By appointment of the nurse here you have been elevated to be my 'family'. I am glad to have acquired a family before I die, my earlier family having all preceded me from this world. To sleep, with my new family nearby, is a wish I would not have had the temerity to make, such a wish goes beyond what is reasonable to expect for myself. Go now, your footsteps will not disturb me. And Arthur will stay.

*   *   *

The little noises that seep in from the corridor. I rub my eyes to stay awake. Mr. Julius' breathing, more shallow than when I first came in. His hand, still a little warmth there. I think he may know I'm holding his hand.

A shudder throughout his frame. A ghastly pause. His breathing starts up again shallower than before, hardly enough to show a movement, up and down, of his shape beneath the covers. A twitch of his lips reminds me how his face twitched when we first talked, that day in the café. He's not conscious, so the nurse told me when she came to check him. But I think he may know I'm here. He's not in pain, the nurse assured me, just slipping away. The night hours slowly pass.

The morning breaks sunny, light streaming through the flowered window curtains. Mr. Julius' hand, still warm in mine. There's a jerking tremor, a trail of saliva escapes from the side of his mouth, slowly dribbling down his chin. I wipe it away with a tissue I pull from the box on the bedside table. The only sign of life a throbbing pulse in his neck. I wait, for his next breath. Nothing. Nor do his eyeballs move from side to side under the shut lids. The pulse in his neck ceases. In the silence of early morning, a larger silence. The small warmth of his hand. As his fingers slacken from mine, that small warmth incongruously remains.

BIBLIOGRAPHY

Badeni, S.(1988) A STRANGER TO HELL Tabb House, Padstow, Cornwall.

Boll, Heinrich Trans. L, Vennevitz(1973) GROUP PORTRAIT WITH LADY
McGraw Hill Book Company.

Brendon, P (2000) THE DARK VALLEY Jonathon Cape, London.

Brewster, E. (1986) VANISHED IN DARKNESS. NeWest Publishers Ltd,
Canada.

Callender, P. (1999) DAYS OF THE CROOKED CROSS Country Books,
Bakewell, Derbyshire

Chomsky, N. (1973) 'The Rule of Force in International Affairs'
in FOR REASONS OF STATE, Fontana Collins.

Dimitrov, G. (1951) 'The Reichstag Fire Trial, Final Speech' in SELECTED
ARTICLES AND SPEECHES. Lawrence and Wishart Ltd, London.

Feynman, R.P. (2000) THE PLEASURE OF FINDING THINGS OUT Allen Lane,
The Penguin Press.

Fleming, G . (1982) HITLER AND THE FINAL SOLUTION.
Oxford University Press

Fucik, J. (1951) REPORT FROM THE GALLOWS. translated by Stephen Jolly,
John Spencer & Co (publishers) Ltd, London

Gilbert, M (2000) NEVER AGAIN Harper Collins (in association with
The Imperial War Museum)

Hart, F. (1981) RETURN TO AUSCHWITZ. Sidgwick and Jackson, London.

Keneally, T. (1982) SCHINDLER'S ARK. Hodder and Stoughton.

Kornreich Gelissen, R. (1997) RENA'S PROMISE. Orion Books Ltd London.

Langbein, H. trans. H. Zohn (English edition)AGAINST ALL HOPE.
Constable and Co.

Levi, P. (1987) trans, R Feldman MOMENTS OF REPRIEVE Abacus
(1985) trans. R. Rosenthal. THE PERIODIC TABLE Abacus
(1987) trans. W. Weaver. THE DROWNED AND THE SAVED Abacus

Marks, J (1993) THE HIDDEN CHILDREN Piatkus

Mountfield, D. (1979) THE PARTISANS. The Hamlyn Publishing Group Ltd.

Plant, R. (1987) THE PINK TRIANGLE. Mainstream Publishing, Edinburgh.

Remarque, E.M. (1957) THE BLACK OBELISK Hutchinson

Todorov, T. Trans. A Denner and A. Pollack.(1999) FACING THE EXTREME
Wiedenfeld and Nicolson

Walter, B. (1947) THEME AND VARIATIONS. Hamish Hamilton.

Wolff, I.R.(1960) Pub for Wiener Library CATALOGUE SERIES 1,
PERSECUTION AND RESISTANCE , Valentine Mitchell

ACKNOWLEDGEMENTS

My wish is to include a range of experiences, recording with equal respect the stories of those caught up in unexpected terror, whether politically, non-politically or religiously motivated, whether named or unnamed, survivors and perished, who created by their struggle against Fascism a reservoir of hope.

As I have indicated in the text, Hermann Langbein's scholarly tome '*Against All Hope*' provides a definitive account of organised resistance, which I have drawn on as a reliable source, supplemented from a range of factual and fictionalised accounts.

Julius Fucik's prison diary has, in translation, provided his account of prison experience.

Bruno Walter's autobiography is the source for the tale of the Mann family's rescue via the underground passages.

Information on the war crimes law used at the Nuremberg trials is based on Noam Chomsky's account.

The post-war uses of Landsberg jail are detailed in an article in '*The Sunday Times*,' October 29th 2000 p26 HITLER'S MEN ATE CAVIAR IN WAR CRIMES JAIL.

Additional information on the role of Jehovah's Witnesses is drawn from the 1996 Video, '*Jehovah's Witnesses Stand Firm Against Nazi Assault*' produced by Watchtower Bible and Tract Society of New York, 25 Columbia Heights, Brooklyn, NY 11201-2483, U.S.A.

Books which have provided information or experiences are credited in the text. Main sources are as listed in the Bibliography.